# Eyewitness
# GREAT
# MUSICIANS

Cannon as featured
in Tchaikovsky's
*1812 Overture*

Beatles yellow
submarine

Johann Sebastian Bach

Saxophone

*Sitar*, or
Indian lute

Perotin's *Christmas
Alleluia*, 13th century

Early form of trumpet

# Eyewitness
# GREAT MUSICIANS

Written by
ROBERT ZIEGLER

Rolling Stones
concert program

Clarinet

African *kora*

Manuscript written by J. S. Bach

St. Basil's Cathedral, Moscow

DK

DK Publishing

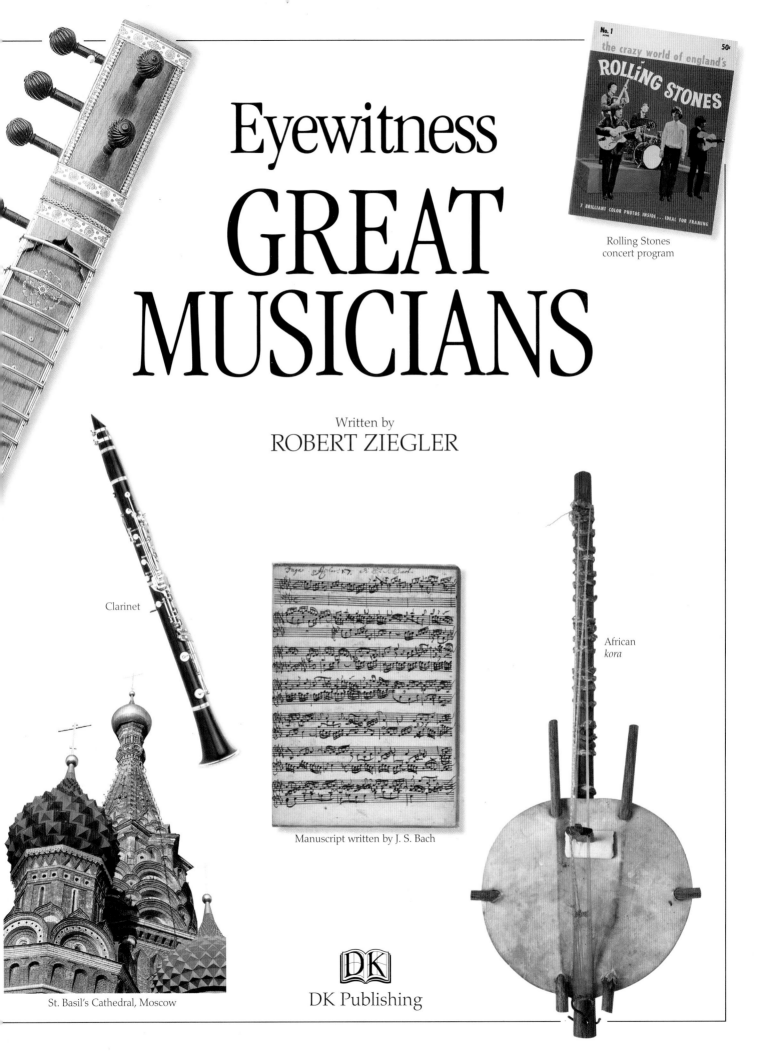

English lute

## LONDON, NEW YORK,
## MELBOURNE, MUNICH, AND DELHI

**Consultant Charles Wiffen**

**Managing editor** Camilla Hallinan
**Managing art editor** Owen Peyton Jones
**Art director** Martin Wilson
**Publishing manager** Sunita Gahir
**Category publisher** Andrea Pinnington
**DK picture library** Claire Bowers, Rose Horridge,
Myriam Megharbi, Kate Shepherd
**Production editor** Hitesh Patel
**Senior production controller** Man Fai Lau
**Jacket designer** Andy Smith
**Jacket editor** John Searcy
**American editor** Christine Heilman

**For Cooling Brown Ltd:**
**Creative Director** Arthur Brown
**Editor** Jemima Dunne
**Designer** Tish Jones
**Picture researcher** Louise Thomas

First published in the United States in 2008 by
DK Publishing,
375 Hudson Street, New York, New York 10014

08 09 10 11 12 10 9 8 7 6 5 4 3 2 1
ED628 – 01/08

Published in Great Britain by Dorling Kindersley Limited

A CIP catalog record for this book
is available from the Library of Congress

ISBN: 978-07566-3774-3 (Hardcover)
978-07566-3773-6 (Library Binding)

Color reproduction by Colourscan, Singapore
Printed and bound in Leo Paper Products Ltd, China

Discover more at
## www.dk.com

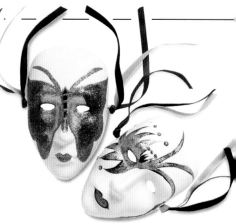

Venetian
carnival masks

Giacomo Puccini

Nutcracker
soldier

Statue of Liberty,
New York

# Contents

Illustrated music manuscript from the Vatican

# Roots of Music

*Sound is created by "flicking" metal strips against wooden board*

*Metal strips are wired on to a soundboard*

African *mbira*, or finger piano

Wʜᴇʀᴇ ᴅɪᴅ ᴍᴜѕɪᴄ ᴄᴏᴍᴇ ғʀᴏᴍ? Nobody knows exactly, because there are no written records. A good guess would be that thousands of years ago, primitive peoples used music in much the same way as we use it now: to communicate, to pass time while working, to express joy or sadness, or to mark a special occasion. The first instrument was the one every person is born with—the body. We have voices to sing and shout with, hands to clap, and feet to stamp. This is enough to create melody and rhythm, the two basic elements of music. Hunters imitated the songs of animals they chased, mothers sang their children to sleep, and tribes rhythmically stamped and shouted to keep away evil spirits. It is a short step from there to making sounds by banging a sticks together or blowing through a hollow reed stalk. So how did we get from there to symphony orchestras and rock stars?

### PREHISTORIC MUSIC LIVES ON
In Africa, music is part of daily life. The *mbira*, or finger piano, is central to the music of Zimbabwe. Instruments like this have been used for thousands of years to communicate with long-dead ancestors, to bring rain during drought, or to stop rain during floods. *Mbira* is also the name given to a type of rhythm music performed by the Shona tribe, which has survived unchanged for thousands of years.

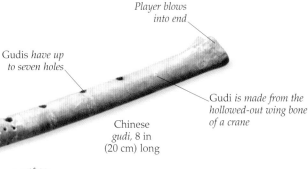

*Player blows into end*

*Gudis have up to seven holes*

*Gudi is made from the hollowed-out wing bone of a crane*

Chinese *gudi*, 8 in (20 cm) long

### MUSIC OF HUNTING
Flutes were among the earliest instruments to be found in all parts of the world. This one, a Chinese *gudi*, dates from around 9000 BCE. It was probably used by hunters to imitate bird sounds. The flute was still playable when it was found in Jiahu, central China, in 1999. Even older flutes dating back 36,000 years have been found in Germany. They tell us that music is as old as humanity.

*Sanctuary of Athena*

Ancient Greek ruins at Delphi

### EARLY SONGS FOR WORSHIP
The world's oldest written song was found in Syria. Carved on stone tablets in about 1400 BCE, it was a hymn to the Moon God's wife to be sung with harp accompaniment. A later song in praise of the Greek god Apollo was found in ancient Greece. It was performed by a boys' choir in 138 BCE at the Pythian Games at Delphi, a forerunner of the Olympics.

*Shofar is made of ram's horn, as a reminder of the ram sacrificed by Abraham*

## ANCIENT INSTRUMENTS

Some of the earliest evidence of ancient music-making comes from statues. This marble carving found at Keros, in the Greek Cyclades islands, shows a person playing type of ancient harp called a lyre. Although it looks modern, it dates back to 2800–2200 BCE, and is one of the oldest statues ever found.

*Each pipe makes a different note*

## REED PIPES

Named after Pan, the Greek god of shepherds, these pan pipes are thought to be among the first instruments ever played. They are made from hollow reeds cut down and tied together. Sound is produced by blowing across one end of the pipes.

## CELEBRATE GOOD TIMES

The *aulos* was a reed instrument similar to the oboe, used in ceremonies and festivals in ancient Egypt, Greece, and the Roman Empire. One legend says that Marsyas the satyr, who played an *aulos*, challenged Apollo, God of music and poetry, to a musical contest. Apollo played the lyre and won.

Egyptian musician playing a double *aulos*

## MUSIC IN WAR

For centuries, music has been used in times of war to inspire troops and terrify the enemy. The Bible says: "If ye go to war… ye shall blow an alarm with the trumpets" (*Book of Numbers 10:9*). The ancient Celts from northern Europe knew this when they blew the *carnyx*, a tall trumpet with a frightening dragon's head that towered over the foot soldiers.

Soldiers with *carnyx* trumpets on a silver cauldron

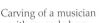

Carving of a musician with an early harp

Rabbi calling with a *shofar*

## MUSIC IN RELIGIOUS CEREMONY

This Jewish ceremonial horn, the *shofar*, is blown in a synagogue on important holy days, such as Rosh Hashanah (New Year) and Yom Kippur (Day of Atonement). It is often mentioned in the Bible: "the exceedingly loud sound of the shofar came down from the clouds on Mount Sinai and made the Israelites tremble in awe" (*Book of Exodus 12:20*).

Jewish *shofar*

# Early Musicians

THE MIDDLE AGES (476–1453 CE) saw the fall of the Roman Empire and the rise of the Catholic Church in Europe, which was crucial to the spread of music through the Western world. The first church music was called plainsong. It was monophonic—just a single tune sung by either one person or a group, mostly from memory before musical notation existed. Throughout this period, secular (nonreligious) music began to flourish, but it was rarely written down. Most of it was performed by minstrels who composed songs about courtly love and accompanied themselves on the lute, the forerunner of the guitar, and the vielle, a kind of violin.

**POLYPHONIC MUSIC**
Music is polyphonic when it has two or more voices, or parts, woven together. At first musicians developed plainsong by adding a second part to the existing single melody. As the practice spread throughout churches, two, three, and four voices were added. One of the earliest composers of this style of music was Pérotin, a French composer who lived in Paris around 1200.

*Each line of notes is sung by a different voice*

Pérotin's *Alleluia nativitas* (Christmas Alleluia)

| | |
|---|---|
| c.1030 | Musical stave described by Guido d'Arezzo (c. 991–c. 1033), using fingers and hand as aids. Also creates solfeggio—the use of the syllables Do-Re-Mi to indicate pitches (notes). |
| 1095 | The First Crusade (religious war) is called for by Pope Urban II to take Jerusalem from the Muslims. |
| 1125 | Rise of troubadours (traveling musicians) in southern France. |
| 1165–1200 | French composers Léonin and Pérotin write music for Notre Dame Cathedral, Paris. |
| 1320 | Publication of Arts Nova, a musical treatise attributed to Philippe de Vitry (1291–1361). |
| 1363 | Guillaume de Machaut (1300–77) composes his Messe de Nostre Dame (Mass for Our Lady). |
| 1430 | Flemish school of music emerges in northern Europe represented by Gilles Binchois (1400–60) and Guillaume Dufay (1397–1474). |
| 1455 | Johannes Gutenberg develops printing with movable type in Germany. |
| 1498 | Music first printed in Venice by Ottaviano Petrucci. |
| 1517 | Protestant Reformation started by Martin Luther. Later, in 1524, he and Johann Walther publish a book of hymns. |
| 1575 | William Byrd and Thomas Tallis granted printing license by England's Queen Elizabeth I. |

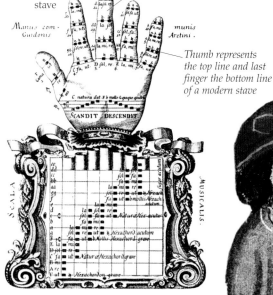

*Guido d'Arezzo's stave*

*System used fingers and a hand to remember music*

*Thumb represents the top line and last finger the bottom line of a modern stave*

**HOW MUSIC NOTATION DEVELOPED**
Music had been written down since 1400 BCE. Guido d'Arezzo (of Arezzo, Italy) was the first person to devise a musical stave (lines and spaces on which music is written). On the stave he indicated pitches (notes) with exact lengths and rhythms. This ended the confusion in the teaching of church music.

*Cornett, an early wooden trumpet*

Hildegard of Bingen (1098–1179)

**SINGING NUN**
Hildegard of Bingen, Germany, is the earliest known female composer. She entered the church at the age of eight and became a nun at 15. This remarkable woman was a religious leader, diplomat, writer, and musician—she left a legacy of over 80 works.

*Vielle*

*Drums*

Group of musicians in an illustrated Bible, 1417

## COMPOSER OF CHURCH MUSIC AND LOVE SONGS

Frenchman Guillaume de Machaut was a priest, poet, and the greatest composer of his time. Unusually, a large amount of his work still exists. He wrote the earliest known complete setting of the Mass, the *Messe de Nostre Dame*, for Rheims Cathedral. He was also a prolific composer of songs about courtly love in the tradition of the troubadours, of ballads using polyphony, and of songs that combined secular texts with sacred melodies.

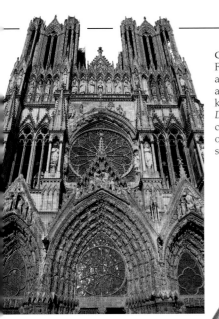

Rheims Cathedral, France

*Medieval triangle*

*Very early lutes had four sets of strings; later ones like this have five or more*

## MEDIEVAL INSTRUMENTS

Musicians in the Middle Ages were great virtuosos (expert soloists) and played an astonishing range of instruments. One of the most popular was the lute, which was a variation on the Arabic *oud*, brought to Europe in the 14th century. Other instruments from the Arab world were the *rebec*, similar to a violin, the *shawm*, an early oboe, and the *cornett*, a long wooden trumpet.

Lute from about 1600

*Early bagpipes*

## MEDIEVAL POPULAR SONG

The Middle Ages had popular singers and songwriters called troubadours. A common image is of a wandering minstrel carrying a lute. More often they were poets supported by the courts or even the aristocrats themselves. Their songs dealt mainly with stories of chivalry and courtly love, but they also carried tales from place to place, like a musical newscast.

*Lute*

## PERMISSION TO PRINT

Composers Thomas Tallis (1505–85), top, and William Byrd (1539–1623) were granted the first license to publish music in England by Queen Elizabeth I. Tallis was a Catholic, yet he served under four English monarchs, from Henry VIII to Elizabeth I, when the state religion was Protestantism. He wrote a famous 40-part work for a choir called *Spem in Alium*.

## SINGING IN CHURCH

Priests and monks sang using polyphonic settings for the Ordinary of the Mass (the parts of a church service that are the same every day). The plainsong melody was set in a strict rhythm, and used as the lowest voice or bass. Above this there were up to three other lines, each given other texts so that different words and rhythms were heard together resonating through the church.

GIOVANNI PIERLUIGI DA
PALESTRINA 1525–94
One of the greatest composers of
Masses (services) for the Roman
Catholic Church, Palestrina is also
famous for writing madrigals—
unaccompanied songs for several
voices—which were popular then.

# Palestrina

ONE OF THE OUTSTANDING COMPOSERS of 16th-century Renaissance
Italy, Palestrina is regarded as a supreme master of counterpoint—music in
which two or more independent melodies are played at the same time
in a way that sounds tuneful. Palestrina spent most of his career as *maestro
di capella* (chorus master) in churches in Rome. He wrote hundreds of
works, both religious and secular, most of which still exist. Palestrina
survived three outbreaks of disease in Italy, but his wife and most of his
family died. Chorus masters were not well paid, but another marriage
to a wealthy merchant, Virginia Dormoli, ensured that
he had enough money to continue composing.

THE VATICAN CITY
The center of the Roman Catholic Church and its music is the
Vatican. Palestrina started out here at the *Cappella Giulia*
(Julian Choir), then at the famous Sistine Chapel. He was
dismissed by Pope Marcellus II for being married. He
became chorus master for other churches in Rome, later
returning to the *Cappella Giulia*, for the rest of his life.

Dome of St. Peter's
Basilica, Vatican Ci

| | |
|---|---|
| c.1525 | Giovanni Pierluigi born in Palestrina, near Rome, Italy. |
| c.1544 | Becomes organist and chorus master in Palestrina. |
| 1547 | Marries Lucrezia Gori. |
| 1550 | Moves to Rome and becomes chorus master of Cappella Giulia. |
| 1554 | Publishes his first book of Masses. |
| 1555 | Appointed to the Sistine Choir. Publishes his first book of madrigals. He is also appointed chorus master at St. John Lateran, the main church in Rome. |
| 1561–66 | Moves to church of Santa Maria Maggiore. |
| 1567 | Publishes Book of Masses, which includes Missa Pape Marcelli, dedicated to Pope Marcellus II. |
| 1571 | Returns to the Cappella Giulia. |
| 1580 | Wife dies in an outbreak of the plague. He marries fur trader Virginia Dormoli a year later. |
| 1594 | February 2, dies in Rome. |

Handwritten music
from the Sistine
Chapel library

POWER OF THE POPES
Palestrina served under 11 popes
during his lifetime, and he saw his
fortunes rise and fall with them. A
former Bishop of Palestrina
became Pope Julius III in
1550. He was Palestrina's
first and greatest patron,
and appointed him as
chorus master to his
*Cappella Giulia*. One of
Palestrina's greatest
works is dedicated to
Julius II's successor,
Pope Marcellus II.

CHANT MUSIC FROM THE VATICAN
The *Cappella Giulia* is still the choir that participates in
all solemn functions in St. Peter's, the largest church
in the Vatican. Its name comes from Pope Julius II,
who reorganized the choir in 1513 and encouraged the
training of Italian musicians. In contrast, members of
the Sistine Chapel Choir were from all over Europe.

Pope Julius II,
founder of the
*Cappella Giulia*

**CLAUDIO MONTEVERDI 1567–1643**
Monteverdi's music marked the transition from the Renaissance to the Baroque period of music (1600–1750). He was a musical revolutionary who developed a simplified, direct style of music that combined voices and instruments to dramatic effect.

# Claudio Monteverdi

MONTEVERDI WAS AMONG the first composers to write what we know today as opera. He developed a dramatic musical language that combined words and action with music to make some of the earliest and greatest musical theater. From the age of 15 until his death, Monteverdi developed his musical style by writing books of madrigals; his most famous collection is *Madrigals of War and Love*. His music used instruments to accompany voices, which was a great innovation at the time. He left his job at the court of the Duke of Mantua to become *maestro di capella* at the grand St. Mark's Basilica in Venice. Monteverdi is thought to have composed his great sacred works, *Vespers for the Blessed Virgin* and his *Mass*, to secure this position.

| | |
|---|---|
| 1567 | May 15, baptized in Cremona, Italy, his birthplace. |
| 1587 | Publishes first of nine books of madrigals. |
| 1590 | Becomes a gamba (early cello) player for Duke of Mantua. |
| 1599 | Marries singer Claudia Cattaneo, daughter of a musician. |
| 1600 | Travels in Austria, Hungary, and Italy as part of Duke's entourage. |
| 1607 | Composes his opera L'Orfeo; wife Claudia dies. Writes his second opera, Arianna, a year later. |
| 1610 | Composes Mass and Vespers for the Blessed Virgin dedicated to Pope Paul V. |
| 1613 | Appointed chorus master at St. Mark's Basilica in Venice, where he remains to the end of his life. |
| 1638 | Publishes Madrigals of Love and War. |
| 1632 | Becomes a Catholic priest. |
| 1643 | November 29, dies in Venice. |

**CREMONA CATHEDRAL**
Monteverdi was born in Cremona, Italy, and received his earliest musical training at the cathedral. The town was an important center of musical instrument making, with the violin-makers Amati, Guarneri, and Stradivari all based there. The music-loving Bishop of Cremona spread the town's fame when he became Pope Gregory XIV in 1590.

Monteverdi's manuscript, *Coronation of Poppea*, 1642

**MONTEVERDI THE REVOLUTIONARY**
One of Monteverdi's most important innovations was assigning specific instruments to accompany singers. He also wrote music that gave prominence to the highest (soprano) and lowest (bass) voices over the other voices, and introduced *pizzicato* (plucking) and *tremolando* (rapid repetition of a note) in string instruments.

*Exotic hand-painted masks are worn for Carnival*

**CARNIVAL OF VENICE**
The tradition of wearing masks during Carnival time in Venice stretches back to 1268. This is a festival of music and entertainment that precedes the Christian holy days of Lent. Monteverdi is thought to have composed the operatic scene *Il Combattimento di Tancredi e Clorinda* for the 1624 Carnival.

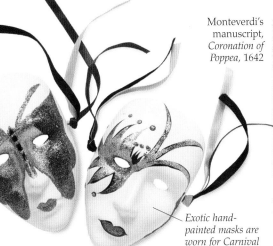

*Jeremy White as Pluto*

*Stephanie Marshall as Proserpina*

**L'ORFEO**
When Monteverdi composed his first opera he created a new genre of music, the *dramma per musica* (musical drama). Its powerful orchestration creates vivid musical pictures of the action on stage. The story is based on the ancient Greek myth about Orpheus, who tries to rescue his dead wife Eurydice from Hades, the underworld. In this scene, Proserpina, the Queen of Hades, is moved by Orfeo's song and persuades Pluto, her King, to free Eurydice.

# George Frideric Handel

**GEORGE FRIDERIC HANDEL**
**1685–1759**
Beethoven emphasized Handel's popular appeal when he said, "Go to him to learn how to achieve great effects, by such simple means." Handel had to be expert at winning over audiences because, in his day, it was customary to eat, play cards, and hold loud conversations during an opera.

| | |
|---|---|
| **1685** | February 23, born in Halle, Germany. His father is a society barber/surgeon and his mother the daughter of a Lutheran pastor. |
| **1702** | Enrolls at Halle University to study law, but switches to music after his father's death. Appointed assistant organist at Halle Cathedral. |
| **1703** | Moves to Hamburg to work at the opera house. |
| **1706** | Travels to Italy; composes opera and his first oratorios. In Italy he performs with an orchestra led by Arcangelo Corelli (1653–1713). |
| **1710** | Returns to Germany and is appointed music director to the Elector of Hanover. |
| **1711** | Makes first trip to London, then settles there a year later. |
| **1717** | Composes Water Music for King George I. |
| **1720** | Appointed musical director of Royal Academy of Music. |
| **1723** | Appointed composer of the King's Chapel Royal; composes opera Giulio Cesare (Julius Caesar). |
| **1742** | Premieres Messiah, the story of Jesus's life, in Dublin, Ireland. |
| **1749** | Performs Music for the Royal Fireworks in London's Green Park. |
| **1751** | Suffers from failing sight, which leads to blindness in 1753. |
| **1759** | Dies; his funeral in Westminster Abbey is attended by 3,000. |

**B**EST KNOWN FOR HIS CHORAL COMPOSITIONS, which became the basis of an entire era of English music, Handel was born in Germany in the same year as Johann Sebastian Bach. In spite of showing considerable musical talent as a boy, he briefly studied the law to please his father, but then he devoted himself to music. He eventually became *Kapellmeister* (music director) to George, Elector of Hanover, later England's King George I. It was in England that Handel enjoyed his greatest successes. His oratorios (dramatic settings of religious texts for orchestra, choir, and soloists) have remained at the heart of English choral tradition since they were first performed. His wrote a staggering 23 oratorios, over 50 operas, and many instrumental works. His most famous pieces are *The Messiah, Music for the Royal Fireworks*, and *Water Music*. At the time, London was a great center of music-making and attracted many other great composers. Handel lived there for over 36 years and his home, 25 Brook Street, is now a museum—the Handel House.

> *"Handel understands effect better than any of us—when he chooses, he strikes like a thunderbolt."*

**WOLFGANG AMADEUS MOZART**
describing the effects of Handel's music to a friend

**HARPSICHORD**
This was one of the indispensable instruments of Baroque music, and a forerunner of the piano. Harpsichords were often used to accompany orchestral and choral works. Before conductors, musicians often directed a performance from the harpsichord, adding improvised (made up) ornamentations or extra melody to the tune. The harpsicord also provided *basso continuo*, or continuous accompaniment. Handel's harpsichord can be seen at the Handel House.

**KING GEORGE I**
George, Elector of Hanover (1660–1727), became King George I of England in 1714 on the death of Queen Anne. Handel wrote his famous *Water Music* for a concert on King George's barge on the Thames River. Handel is seen in the center of the painting, presenting the music to the King, who is seated in the shade. The King liked the piece so much that he requested three more performances; the exhausted musicians went home at three in the morning.

*On main keyboard, each key links to a string*

## CORONATION MUSIC

Handel's career was closely bound up with events at the English court—he was asked to write many pieces for royal occasions. His anthem, *Zadok the Priest*, is one of four anthems (short choral pieces) composed for the coronation of King George II (George I's son) in 1727, has been sung at the coronation of every British monarch since. It is also the anthem for the UEFA Champions League soccer matches.

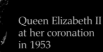

Queen Elizabeth II at her coronation in 1953

## FAMOUS FIREWORKS

King George II asked Handel for music to accompany a huge fireworks display in London. The music had to be very loud, so Handel wrote it for a colossal orchestra that included 24 oboes, 12 bassoons, nine horns, nine trumpets, and three kettledrums. Handel was so popular that over 12,000 people attended the rehearsal. The fireworks won in the end, as the building the musicians were performing in caught fire.

## MESSIAH

Written in 1741, the *Messiah* remains the most popular oratorio, with its instantly recognizable "Hallelujah" chorus. Handel wrote it in three weeks without ever leaving his house. In order to have enough room for the huge audience at the premiere, gentlemen were asked to leave their swords at home.

Handel's original score for the *Messiah*

*Strings are plucked by quills (unlike piano strings, which are "hit" with hammers)*

Antonio Vivaldi
(1648–1741)

*Keys on second keyboard connect to separate strings*

## ANTONIO VIVALDI

Vivaldi was an Italian contemporary of Handel. Like Handel, he wrote many Baroque operas (over 55 in all). He was a brilliant virtuoso violinist, and knew how to achieve sparkling effects in writing for stringed instruments. Vivaldi wrote more than 520 concertos (works for soloist and orchestra)—his most famous is *The Four Seasons*. Many of his works were premiered at the girls' orphanage in Venice where he was violin teacher.

# Johann Sebastian Bach

**JOHANN SEBASTIAN BACH**
**(1685–1750)**
Bach was a violinist, organist, choir master, harpsichordist, teacher, and composer. He was immensely gifted, but said of his gifts: "I am obliged to work hard. Whoever is equally industrious will achieve just as well."

| | |
|---|---|
| 1685 | *March 21, born in Eisenach, Germany. His father and uncles provide early instruction in violin, harpsichord, and organ.* |
| 1694-5 | *Mother dies, followed by his father. Bach goes to live with his eldest brother, Johann Christoph (1671–1721), organist at nearby Ohrdruf.* |
| 1700 | *Awarded choral scholarship to study in Lüneberg.* |
| 1703 | *Becomes violinist in Court Orchestra of the Duke of Weimar. After seven months, he leaves to become organist in Arnstadt.* |
| 1707 | *Takes up post of organist in Mühlhausen and marries second cousin, Maria Barbara Bach.* |
| 1717 | *Becomes Kapellmeister (music director) at court of Prince Leopold of Anhalt-Cöthen. Composes the "Brandenburg" concertos here.* |
| 1723 | *Appointed Kantor (chorus master) of St. Thomas's Church and the Thomasschule (school) in Leipzig.* |
| 1729 | *Becomes director of the Collegium Musicum; his St. Matthew Passion is first performed.* |
| 1747 | *With failing eyesight, he visits his son C. P. E. Bach in Potsdam. Here he improvises on a theme suggested by King Frederick the Great, which results in A Musical Offering.* |
| 1749 | *Completes Mass in B Minor and The Art of Fugue.* |
| 1750 | *Dies following an eye operation. Buried in St. Thomas's Church.* |

FAMOUS IN HIS LIFETIME for his incredible keyboard skills and genius at improvising music, Bach wrote more than 1,000 works, ranging from solo violin pieces to works for full chorus, soloists, organ, and orchestra. His compositions stand unchallenged as the high point of the Baroque period of music, when elaborate polyphonic music was the ideal. In his lifetime, Bach was admired by great musicians including Handel, Mozart, and Beethoven. He was also criticized by some for writing music that was considered overly complicated. Immediately after his death, Bach's work was overlooked in favor of simpler music styles that had become more fashionable.

**FAMILY MAN**
Bach had 20 children—seven from his first marriage (his first wife died in 1721), another 13 with his second wife, Anna Magdalena. Several of his children also had distinguished musical careers—in particular: Wilhelm Friedemann (1710–84), Carl Philipp Emanuel (1714–88), and the youngest, Johann Christian (1735–82), who was also known as the "London" Bach because of the time he spent there. However, fewer than half of J. S. Bach's children outlived him.

*Choristers from the world-famous King's College Choir, Cambridge*

**CHURCH CHOIRS**
In Bach's time, church choirs only had male voices—young boys to sing the high parts and older boys and men for the lower ones. There were about 50 boys in Bach's choir, but they were shared among four churches. Since Bach's busy choir provided music for weddings, funerals, and graduations, as well as normal church services, the boys had to sing several times a day.

**MARTIN LUTHER**
Luther (1483–1546) was a German monk who protested against abuses of power in the Roman Catholic Church. He translated the Bible into German to make it more accessible to people. Luther also composed many hymns. Bach used Luther's Bible and hymns in his cantatas—pieces sung by soloists and the choir in a church service. Bach wrote over 200 cantatas, enough for five years of Sundays.

> *"For the glory of the most high God alone, And for my neighbor to learn from."*
>
> **BACH**
> The epigraph to his *Little Organ Book,* 1713

Forested mountains on Bach's walk through northern Germany

**GREATEST PRODUCTIVITY**
Bach was chorus master at St. Thomas's Church for years, and he wrote many of his most important works there. He taught singing at the *Thomasschule,* producing weekly music for this and other nearby churches. He became director of the *Collegium Musicum,* an instrumental group that performed his concertos (music for solo instruments accompanied by an orchestra).

St. Thomas's Church, Leipzig

**WALK OF A LIFETIME**
Imagine going to visit a musical hero and asking him or her for a lesson. That is what Bach did when he left his job in Arnstadt for several months in 1705–06 in order to visit a famous organist, Dieterich Buxtehude (c. 1637–1707), in the northern city of Lübeck. Determined to make the trip, the young Bach walked the 250 miles (400 km) across the mountains to Lübeck and back.

**MUSIC FOR KEYBOARD**
Playing Bach's music helps anyone improve their technique and composition skills. Bach wrote works at many levels— from the elementary, such as his *Notebook for Anna Magdalena* (his second wife), to major pieces that challenge soloists like András Schiff. Hungarian-born Schiff is one of the greatest living interpreters of Bach's music.

András Schiff (b. 1953)

**DRAMATIC ORGAN COMPOSITIONS**
Organs were central to Bach's music. He composed many organ pieces, some of which were to be performed by choir, orchestra, and organ together. Many of his most important works were based on melodies sung in church services. Bach originally made his reputation on his phenomenal ability to improvise at the organ. Early in his career, Bach got into trouble for improvising so wildly that he confused the people trying to sing along in church.

*Pipe organs were a feature in the churches where Bach worked*

# Franz Joseph Haydn

FRANZ JOSEPH HAYDN (1732–1809)
Haydn led an amazingly productive life, composing over 1,000 pieces in all. Although it was customary to treat musicians as servants, his music-loving employers gave him enough time to compose, and his fame spread throughout Europe.

| | |
|---|---|
| 1732 | *March 31, born in village of Rohrau, Austria.* |
| 1738 | *Sent to live in Hainburg to begin musical training with a relative.* |
| 1740 | *Becomes a chorister at St. Stephen's Cathedral, Vienna.* |
| 1753 | *Starts to work as accompanist and apprentice to singer Nicola Porpora.* |
| 1759 | *Composes his Symphony No. 1.* |
| 1760 | *Marries Maria Keller, but they later separate.* |
| 1761 | *Becomes deputy Kapellmeister (music director) at Prince Esterházy's court; later becomes director.* |
| 1765 | *Writes Cello Concerto No. 1.* |
| 1772 | *First performance of the Farewell Symphony; musicians famously leave the stage one by one.* |
| 1790 | *Prince Nikolaus Esterházy dies. A year later Haydn visits England, staying for 18 months. Composes six symphonies, including his Surprise Symphony.* |
| 1792 | *Meets and teaches the young Beethoven for a short time.* |
| 1795 | *Commissioned to write The Creation on his second visit to England. It is performed in 1798 in Vienna, and London in 1799.* |
| 1795 | *Returns to the Esterházy court and focuses on church music.* |
| 1802 | *Is seriously ill, so stops composing. Dies in Vienna, May 1809.* |

HAYDN IS THE COMPOSER who did more than any other to create the Classical style of music, which emphasizes melody and harmony over polyphony. It gave rise to new musical forms that enabled composers to tell musical "stories"—in particular, they developed the symphony to do this. A symphony is a large work with three or four sections called movements, and it uses some Baroque musical forms within it, especially dances, such as minuets. It took many years and many composers to create this new music. Haydn is known as the "Father of the Symphony," and he wrote over 100 such works. He also wrote more than 700 pieces of chamber music—music for small ensembles, or groups, like string quartets. He was employed for most of his life at the Esterházy court in Hungary, which meant that he was isolated from the large musical centers of the time, such as Vienna. This forced him to develop his own distinctive style.

Scale model of the theater at the Esterházy Palace

*Viola*    *Cellist*    *Second violin*

*First violin*

THE STRING QUARTET
Chamber groups of four string instruments, two violins (a first and second), a viola, and a cello, have proved attractive to composers two centuries. At first, Haydn wrote light music (called *divertimentos* or serenades) for string quartets, for entertaining at court. Gradually he began to write more serious music for them as well. In all, he wrote 68 quartets.

MODERN MUSICIAN
Haydn's symphonies are a key part of the repertoire of modern orchestras and smaller ensembles that play on authentic 18th-century instruments. The modern orchestra makes a more uniform sound; the older instruments have an exciting earthiness. The English conductor Simon Rattle, seen here, directs both kinds of groups.

ESTERHÁZY PALACE THEATRE
Haydn was employed by Prince Nikolaus von Esterházy for nearly 30 years as his music director or *Kapellmeister*. Fortunately, the Prince was a great lover of music and gave him daily access to a small orchestra. In return, Haydn ran the orchestra, played and composed chamber music, and wrote Masses for the Court's church and operas for its theater.

Simon Rattle conducting the Berlin Philharmonic Orchestra

*Weidinger's keyed trumpet*

### NEW TRUMPET, NEW WORKS
Even late in his life, Haydn was still finding new challenges. In 1796 he wrote a concerto for Anton Weidinger's new "keyed" trumpet, which offered a greater range of notes than the earlier instrument. Haydn's last years were full of great works, including his *Nelson Mass* (1798), completed soon after the British Admiral Horatio Nelson defeated the French Emperor Napoleon in the Battle of the Nile.

### HAYDN GOES TO ENGLAND
After Prince Nikolaus' death, Haydn was invited to London by a concert promoter. While there, he produced some of his most memorable named symphonies, such as the *Surprise*, *Military*, and *London* symphonies. A storm on his trip across the English Channel was said to have inspired his great oratorio, *The Creation*.

> *"My Prince was always satisfied… and I was in a position to improve, alter, and be as bold as I pleased."*

**HAYDN**
writing about his employer,
Prince Nikolaus Esterházy

*Lavish music productions were a feature of court life*

*Orchestra in Haydn's day could be seen by the audience*

### FOLK MUSIC
Haydn's mother was a cook and his father a wheelwright. Both were very musical, and enjoyed Bohemian folk music. Haydn heard many folk songs as a boy, and often used a them as the theme for a rousing finale (end) to his symphonies or string quartets. He also used folk music from other parts of Europe.

*Mozart's dedication letter to Haydn*

### MUSICAL FRIENDSHIP
Although Haydn was 24 years older than Mozart, the two were close friends and enjoyed playing in string quartets together. As a sign of his friendship, Mozart dedicated a set of six string quartets (written 1782–85) to Haydn. In his letter, he offers "the fruits of long and laborious endeavor [*to my*] most dear friend."

# Wolfgang Amadeus Mozart

**WOLFGANG AMADEUS MOZART (1756–91)**
One of the most inspired composers ever, Mozart is repeatedly voted the most popular composer. His output of over 600 compositions includes works widely acknowledged as pinnacles of symphonic, chamber, piano, operatic, and choral music. Dozens of his works are still part of the standard repertoire.

THIS UNIVERSALLY LOVED GENIUS had an early musical start. At the urging of his father, also a musician, Mozart began composing at the age of four. He spent much of his childhood and teenage years touring Europe as a virtuoso pianist prodigy. These travels gave the young Mozart invaluable exposure to the musical styles being played in cities as far apart as Vienna, Prague, Mannheim, Paris, and London. Mozart was a musical "sponge," soaking up music wherever he went. Most famously, after hearing a performance of Gregorio Allegri's *Miserere* in the Sistine Chapel in Rome—a complicated piece for two choirs that had never been sung outside the Vatican—the 14-year-old Mozart went home and wrote the music out from memory.

| | |
|---|---|
| 1756 | *January 27, born in Salzburg, Austria. Father Leopold is a composer and court musician.* |
| 1764 | *Composes first Symphony.* |
| 1768 | *Opera* Bastien and Bastienne *is staged.* |
| 1772 | *Appointed* Konzertmeister (*music director*) *at Salzburg.* |
| 1773 | *Fails to gain job in Vienna. Composes motet* Exsultate, Jubilate, *many string quartets, and symphonies.* |
| 1778 | *Travels with his mother to Paris, where she dies. Writes* Paris Symphony *and* Concerto for Flute and Harp. |
| 1782 | *Marries singer Constanze Weber. Begins string quartets dedicated to his friend Haydn.* |
| 1786 | *Premieres* The Marriage of Figaro, *and composes* Piano Concertos No. 23 *to* 25, *and the* Prague Symphony. |
| 1787 | *Visits Prague twice: premieres* Prague Symphony *and* Don Giovanni *while there.* |
| 1788 | *Has severe money problems. Composes his three greatest symphonies in six weeks (Nos. 39, 40, and 41).* |
| 1791 | *Writes* The Magic Flute *and his* Clarinet Concerto. *Dies before completing* Requiem, *and is buried in an unmarked grave.* |

**MOZART'S MUSIC LESSONS**
When Mozart was three, his seven-year-old sister, Maria Anna, known as Nannerl, was given piano lessons. Mozart was very eager to join in. His father, Leopold, obliged, and was impressed with his son's speedy progress. Imagine his surprise when Mozart then demonstrated his ability to play the violin, which he had learned without his father's knowledge.

*"He is the only musician who had as much knowledge as genius, and as much genius as knowledge."*

**GIOACCHINO ROSSINI (1792–1868)**
Italian composer, describing Mozart's work

Papageno, the birdcatcher in *The Magic Flute*

**CHILD PRODIGY**
From the time Mozart was six until he was thirteen, he traveled around Europe on concert tours with his father and sister. While in London, Leopold became very ill. The children were forbidden to touch the piano as it would wake their father. To occupy himself, the eight-year-old Mozart composed his first symphony.

Mozart's first violin

Mozart performing at the piano with his father and sister

Maxim Vengerov (b. 1974)

**VIOLIN VIRTUOSOS**
Mozart was described by his father as a "miracle which God let be born in Salzburg." He is still a favorite son of the city. In his teens, Mozart became a court musician for the Archbishop and composed five violin concertos. Violin virtuosos, such as the Russian Maxim Vengerov, relish the challenge of playing these concertos.

## WIND INSTRUMENTS
Mozart had a special affection for wind instruments, and he gave them a prominent role in his operas and symphonies. He also wrote many serenades to be performed outdoors—open-air performance is especially effective for wind instruments. Perhaps the greatest serenade is the *Gran Partita* for 13 wind instruments, written in 1780.

18th-century bassoon player

*Teddy Tahu Rhodes as Don Giovanni*

## IMPORTANT OPERA COMPOSER
Mozart wrote 22 operas, but the most popular are those he wrote with the poet Lorenzo da Ponte (1749–1838). These are: *Don Giovanni*, based on the famous "Don Juan" legend; *The Marriage of Figaro;* and *Cosi fan tutte,* which means "women are all like that." Each opera marries comedy, intrigue, and emotion with beautiful music.

*Richard Alexander as Leporello*

*Don Giovanni* at the Opera House in Sydney, Australia

Tom Hulce as Mozart in the 1984 film *Amadeus*

## AMADEUS
Mozart's extraordinary life inspired the play *Amadeus* by Peter Shaffer. The play portrays Mozart as a high-spirited prankster, an 18th-century pop star who composes music of unspeakable beauty with little effort. This is much to the frustration of Mozart's rival composer at court, Antonio Salieri (1750–1825).

## THE MAGIC FLUTE
*The Magic Flute* is a *singspiel*—an opera that combines singing with spoken dialogue. Mozart wrote it in 1791 for a friend's Viennese theater company. Its fantastical story involves a prince's search for an imprisoned princess. The prince fights a serpent, meets a birdcatcher who plays the pipes, and finally meets his princess. There is also an evil Queen of the Night who sings one of the highest notes in opera—F6.

*Mozart's notes enabled his student to complete the piece*

## LAST WORDS
The *Requiem*, which was completed after Mozart's death by his student Süssmayer, is surrounded by mystery. It was commissioned by a patron who asked to remain anonymous. In 1791, Mozart, in poor health, struggled unsuccessfully to finish it. The cause of his death at only 36 was unclear. This gave rise to the famous, but unfounded, rumor that he was killed by a jealous rival.

Mozart's notebook for his *Requiem*

# Ludwig van Beethoven

**LUDWIG VAN BEETHOVEN (1770–1827)**
Beethoven's father was his first teacher. His work marks the crossover between the Classical and Romantic periods when composers wrote more emotional music. Beethoven's work has three distinct periods: early, middle (when he was losing his hearing), and late (by which time he was completely deaf).

BEETHOVEN IS ONE OF THE most important figures in Western music. He composed some of the most astonishing music ever written, but had a troubled life. He was plagued by hearing problems from a very early age. While still a boy, he supported his family as a traveling performer. At the age of 17 he impressed Mozart in Vienna, Austria, and moved there to study with Haydn. He amazed many people in high social circles with his piano playing. The musical visions expressed in his many symphonies, piano compositions, and string quartets were often far ahead of their time, and sometimes left the audience bewildered. He was held in awe by his musical contemporaries.

| | |
|---|---|
| 1770 | December 16, baptized in Bonn, Germany. |
| 1781 | Takes music lessons on violin and organ. |
| 1778 | First public performance in Cologne, Germany, at age six. |
| 1783 | Composes Three Sonatas. |
| 1787 | Studies briefly in Vienna with Mozart. |
| 1792 | Moves to Vienna permanently to study with Joseph Haydn. |
| 1795 | Performs his First Piano Concerto at his first public concert in Vienna. |
| 1799 | Publishes his Pathétique piano sonata. |
| 1802 | Depressed by failing hearing, writes Heiligenstadt Testament. Composes Symphony No. 2 and Kreutzer Violin Sonata. |
| 1804 | Completes Symphony No. 3, The Eroica. |
| 1805 | Premieres his opera Fidelio; he later revises it and the new version is performed in 1814. |
| 1806 | Writes Violin Concerto in D. |
| 1808 | Premieres Symphonies No. 5 and 6 and Piano Concerto No. 4 together in four-hour concert. |
| 1822 | Completes Symphony No. 9, and Diabelli Variations for piano a year later. |
| 1827 | Dies in Vienna; 10,000 people attend his funeral. |

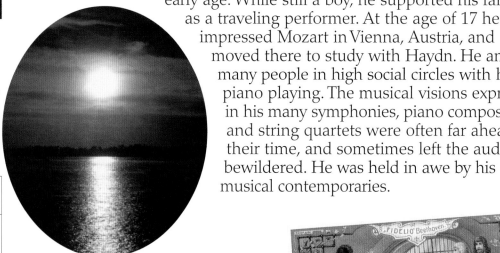

**BEETHOVEN'S EARLY WORKS**
During his early years, Beethoven was always exploring new directions and transforming Classical music into something more dynamic and powerful. Each new work was a struggle, and he sometimes spent years on a piece. Among his most famous early works are two piano sonatas: the *Pathétique* (meaning passionate) and *Moonlight* sonatas.

Scene from *Fidelio*, where Leonora reveals her disguise

**"HEROIC" MIDDLE PERIOD**
Despite Beethoven's deafness, this period (1803–14) includes some of his greatest work. Many of the pieces have a heroic atmosphere. They include his *Symphony No. 5* (with its famous *da da da daaaa* opening) and his opera *Fidelio*, which follows the exploits of Leonora, who disguises herself as a prison guard to defy a corrupt governor and free her jailed husband.

Page from Beethoven's conversation books

**BEETHOVEN'S EAR TRUMPETS**
In 1803. Beethoven realized the seriousness of his growing deafness. In his despair he wrote his famous *Heiligenstadt Testament*, in which he resolved to pursue his artistic destiny in spite of losing his hearing. Beethoven used these primitive hearing aids and later relied on "conversation books" to communicate with friends, but found it increasingly difficult to perform.

*Sound resonated in the cup-shaped end*

## SUMMER RESIDENCE
There is evidence that Beethoven lived in more than 60 different places during his 35 years in Vienna. He loved nature deeply, as you can hear in his *Symphony No. 6*, the *Pastoral Symphony*. During the summers he often went to this country house in Baden. While here, he also worked on his last symphony, *Symphony No. 9*.

Rudolf of Habsburg, Archduke of Austria

## PATRONS
Beethoven was an early "freelance" musician who, instead of working for one person, supported himself through a combination of public concerts, sale of his compositions, gifts, and encouragement from wealthy Viennese society patrons. In 1808, Archduke Rudolf granted him an annuity (salary).

*Rudolf in his robes as a Cardinal*

## BEETHOVEN'S LAST WORKS
Although increasingly isolated by his deafness, Beethoven grew bolder and more adventurous as a composer. The crowning achievement of his last years was *Symphony No. 9*, the *Choral Symphony*. For the first time in the history of the symphony, Beethoven used a choir and four vocal soloists to perform his setting of Schiller's *Ode to Joy*—a monumental cry for brotherhood among people.

*Symphony No. 9 conducted by Leonard Slatkin*

Beethoven's hearing instruments, made by Johann Mälzel, inventor of the metronome

*Wire was hooked around the ear*

*This end was held to the ear*

*"I want to seize fate by the throat."*

**BEETHOVEN**
in a letter to his friend, Doctor F. G. Wegeler,
November 16, 1816

## AUTHENTIC ORCHESTRAS
Musical instruments sounded very different in Beethoven's time. Violins had softer strings, the wind and brass instruments were not as powerful, and the concert rooms were smaller. Many of the intimate details of performance have been rediscovered from the composer's notes by conductors like Austrian Nikolaus Harnoncourt. Now we can hear the music as Beethoven's audiences would have heard it.

*English Broadwood piano*

Nikolaus Harnoncourt (b. 1929)

## BEETHOVEN'S PIANO
Beethoven's early success in Vienna was based on his gifts for improvisation at the piano. He wrote 32 piano sonatas (pieces for one instrument with several sections, or movements) and five piano concertos, which made new demands on the instrument. He preferred the strong sound of the English Broadwood, which suited his energetic style; the company gave him one in 1817.

# Franz Liszt

**FRANZ LISZT (1811–86)**
Liszt was a flamboyant, handsome Hungarian who embodied two very different personalities. There was Liszt the wild, almost devil-like, virtuoso pianist and visionary composer with a fanatical following, and Liszt the humble religious man whose only goal was to praise God.

| | |
|---|---|
| 1811 | October 22, born in Dobojan, Hungary; son of Adam Liszt, a minor official for Prince Esterházy and an amateur pianist and cellist. |
| 1821 | Studies with Beethoven's pupil Carl Czerny (1791–1857). |
| 1822 | Gives first public concert in Vienna. |
| 1831 | First hears Paganini play violin and resolves to create same effect with the piano. |
| 1833 | Transcribes Hector Berlioz's (1803–69) Symphonie Fantastique for piano. |
| 1835 | Runs away to Switzerland with Countess Marie d'Agoult. |
| 1839 | Begins performing again; travels on concert tours for eight years. |
| 1847 | Retires from touring, and becomes Kapellmeister (music director) to Duke of Weimar. |
| 1850 | Directs first production of Lohengrin for his friend Wagner, who is exiled from Germany. |
| 1853 | Composes Sonata in B Minor, one of the greatest works for solo piano. |
| 1857 | Premieres his Faust Symphony in Weimar. |
| 1861 | Moves to Rome, where he composes first Mephisto Waltz. |
| 1865 | Becomes an abbé (priest). |
| 1886 | Dies in Bayreuth after attending performances of Wagner's Parsifal and Tristan. |

THE GREATEST PIANIST OF HIS AGE, and possibly of all time, Liszt revolutionized piano playing through his astonishing technique. But Liszt's showmanship captivated his public just as much as his music. He traveled all over Europe performing to huge audiences. Liszt was also renowned for his conducting and his demanding compositions. He coined the term "symphonic poem" for a piece of music based on a dramatic play or historical event. He seemed to have a fascination with the infernal: his *Faust Symphony* is a story about a deal with the Devil; his *Mephisto Waltzes* are also named after the *Devil*; and the *Dante Symphony* was inspired by Dante's *Inferno*, a poem about Hell. The public was spellbound—was he a musician or a magician?

*Liszt at the Piano*
by Josef Danhauser
(1805-45)

**CELEBRATED SOCIETY PERFORMER**
Liszt's flamboyant performances created a wave of "Lisztomania" that swept across Europe. He inspired composers and writers, and in turn was influenced by them. Liszt is seen here at the piano in 1840 surrounded by: (standing from left) writers Alexandre Dumas (*Three Musketeers*), Victor Hugo (*Les Misérables*), and (seated) Paganini, composer Gioacchino Rossini (*William Tell*), and writer George Sand.

Nicolò Paganini (1782–1840)

*Piano keyboards have seven sets of eight notes (octaves); before Liszt they only had five*

**PAGANINI THE PERFORMER**
When Liszt first heard the great violinist Paganini, he was enthralled by his technique. Inspired by this, Liszt went on to create the same fiery effects on the piano. Paganini impressed audiences so much that, with his deathly pale appearance and his extremely long fingers, they suspected he, like Liszt, was in league with the Devil.

*Pedals prolong the sound of a note*

C.BECHSTEIN

## SERGEI RACHMANINOV

Rachmaninov (1873–1943) was a Russian pianist, conductor, and composer. He was very like Liszt, in terms of the staggering virtuosity of his output—four piano concertos, three symphonies, and many solo piano works. His most famous piece is the *Rhapsody on a Theme of Paganini*. This was based on Paganini's *Caprice No. 24*, which was also successfully recycled by Brahms and, more recently, by Andrew Lloyd Webber.

Rachmaninov performing at a concert

Liszt medal awarded by Hungarian Ministry of Culture

## INFLUENCE LIVES ON

Liszt is a Hungarian national hero, and the government awards the Liszt Medal of Honor for outstanding achievements by pianists who perform or record a great deal of his music. Australian pianist Leslie Howard (b. 1948) has received an award for recording all of Liszt's piano music on 94 CDs, for which he won a place in the *Guinness Book of Records*.

## FIRST PIANO RECITALS

A recital is a kind of dramatic presentation before a seated, hushed audience who focus on the performers. In spite of fine recital music written by Mozart and Beethoven, the piano recital did not exist before Liszt—he is credited with inventing it to show off his superstar status. Liszt was also the first to raise the piano lid and turn the open side toward the audience.

Bechstein grand pianoforte

*Lid is raised for recitals, to direct the sound toward the audience*

## *"Devil of a fellow— such a young rascal!"*

**LUDWIG VAN BEETHOVEN**
after hearing the 11-year-old Liszt performing in Vienna

## MUSICAL FAMILY

Liszt had three children. The youngest, Cosima, became deeply involved with music. She married one of the great conductors and champions of Wagner's music, Hans von Bülow (1830–94). She eventually left him and married Wagner himself. Cosima helped Wagner establish his opera house at Bayreuth, and became director of the Bayreuth opera festival after his death.

Cosima Liszt (1837–1930)

## DEVOTION TO THE CHURCH

Liszt finally tired of the exhausting life of a traveling virtuoso and of fawning fans grabbing at his clothes. He settled in Rome, where he took holy orders in the Roman Catholic Church. He still composed and taught, often for free. He selflessly assisted many musicians financially, and helped raise funds for a monument to his hero, Beethoven.

St. John Lateran, the main Roman Catholic Church of the city of Rome

**RICHARD WAGNER (1813–83)**
Wagner was a hugely influential writer and musician. He was very involved in left-wing politics and was eventually expelled from Germany, living in exile for 12 years. He ran up huge debts, which were eventually paid off by King Ludwig II of Bavaria, who became Wagner's patron.

# Richard Wagner

WAGNER WAS A MUSICAL INNOVATOR who revolutionized opera by creating vast music-dramas for which he wrote both the music *and* the words—previously composers had used stories written by librettists. Wagner wanted to create a combination of all the arts—music, poetry, drama, and painting—which he called a *Gesamtkunstwerk*. In addition, each major character, symbol, or place in his dramas had its individual musical theme, or *leitmotif*, that accompanied it throughout the opera. The greatest use of this technique came in his *Ring Cycle*, an epic story told over four operas. Wagner's music was both fiercely criticized and wildly praised in his lifetime. Even now, people have very strong views about his music.

*Wagner's tuba is long and ova[...] unlike the modern ones*

Wagner tuba

**MUSICAL INVENTOR**
Wagner's innovations were not confined to the stage. He also enlarged the orchestra and added new instruments. A blacksmith's anvil hit with a hammer is used in his opera *Siegfried*. A new instrument—the "Wagner tuba"—provided a bass (lower sound) for the trumpet and trombone section, before the modern tuba became a fixture in the orchestra.

| | |
|---|---|
| 1813 | *May 22, born in Leipzig, Germany. Educated in Dresden and Leipzig at Bach's* Thomasschule. |
| 1836 | *Marries Minna Planer. Becomes opera director in Riga, Latvia.* |
| 1839 | *Leaves Riga for London, then Paris because of debts. Writes articles and arranges other composers' works. Writes* Rienzi *and* Der Fliegende Holländer *(The Flying Dutchman).* |
| 1845 | Tannhäuser *staged in Dresden.* |
| 1849 | *Joins Dresden Uprising against the Kingdom of Saxony for freedom of the press, self-organization of universities, and independent Parliament; flees to Weimar, then to Zurich, Switzerland.* |
| 1854-7 | *Completes two operas of his Ring Cycle—Das Rheingold and Die Walküre—and part of* Siegfried. |
| 1863 | *Falls in love with Franz Liszt's daughter, Cosima.* |
| 1864 | *Ludwig II becomes king of Bavaria and Wagner's patron.* |
| 1865 | *Hans von Bülow conducts* Tristan und Isolde *in Munich.* |
| 1866 | *Wife dies. Wagner marries Cosima four years later.* |
| 1867 | *Completes opera* Die Meistersinger von Nürnberg. |
| 1872 | *Moves to Bayreuth with Cosima. Opens the* Festspielhaus *in 1876.* |
| 1883 | *Dies in Venice. Liszt writes* La Lugubre Gondola *for him.* |

**THE RING OF NIBELUNGEN (*DER RING DES NIBELUNGEN*)**
The *Ring Cycle* is Wagner's major work. The story revolves around a magic ring that grants power to rule the world. A dwarf, Alberich, made the ring from gold stolen from the Rheinmaidens (mermaids from the Rhine River). Over the course of four operas (*Das Rheingold, Die Walküre, Siegfried*, and *Götterdämmerung*), gods, giants, dragons, and heroes struggle for possession of the magic ring.

The Rheinmaidens in *Götterdämmerung*, at London's Royal Opera House, 2006

Poster for Wagner's *Parsifal*, by Heinz Pinggora (1813–83)

**PARSIFAL**
Wagner's final opera, *Parsifal*, was first performed in 1882. It is a beautiful story about innocence, compassion, charity, and faith. Wagner was fascinated with myths and legends. Here he draws on the legends of King Arthur to create a tale of a hero, Parsifal, who is taken on a journey to find the sacred spear to cure a dying king.

## FAMILIAR MUSIC
The famous wedding march *Here Comes the Bride* is from Wagner's opera *Lohengrin*, which was directed in 1850 by his friend Franz Liszt. Many filmmakers and composers also fell under Wagner's spell. Director Fritz Lang (1890–1976) made an early silent film of the ring legend called *Nibelungen*. The music from the *Ride of the Valkyries*, from the opera *Die Walküre*, features in many films.

## BAYREUTH'S FESTSPIELHAUS
Wagner's demands for presenting his operas extended to dimming the lights and placing the orchestra in a sunken "pit"—both unusual at the time, but now standard. With the help of King Ludwig II, Wagner built an opera house devoted to the performance of his works. The *Festspielhaus* opened in 1876 with the first performance of the *Ring Cycle*. The annual Bayreuth Festival at the *Festspielhaus* is a celebration of Wagner's operas.

## HERBERT VON KARAJAN
Wagner was a revolutionary conductor. In his essay *On Conducting* (1869), he proposed that a creative conductor should actively interpret music, rather than just control an orchestra like a traffic cop. Many conductors have followed his example, including his disciple Hans von Bülow (1830–94), and the great Herbert von Karajan (1908–89).

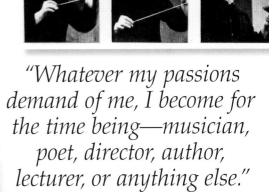

> "Whatever my passions demand of me, I become for the time being—musician, poet, director, author, lecturer, or anything else."

**WAGNER**
in a letter to Franz Liszt, his great friend

## NAZI FOLLOWING
Adolf Hitler (1889–1945), leader of the German Nazi party, was a great admirer of Wagner. Hitler felt that the heroic aspirations of his Third Reich (empire) were embodied in the epic mythology of Wagner's operas. Joseph Goebbels, Hitler's Propaganda Minister, took images from the *Ring Cycle* to portray the Nazi party as truth-seeking heroes protecting the German nation.

Hitler on a magazine cover, 1935

# Giuseppe Verdi

**GIUSEPPE VERDI (1813–1901)**
Verdi, born in the same year as Wagner, composed opera all his life. Verdi was a political musician, and many of his works reflect the nationalist movement in Italy at the time, the *Risorgimento*.

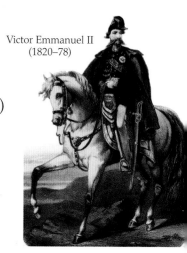

Victor Emmanuel II (1820–78)

**I**TALY'S GREATEST OPERA COMPOSER is Giuseppe Verdi (which translates as "Joe Green") and his music is part of Italian culture. Great *arias* (songs) such as *La Donna é Mobile* (from *Rigoletto*) or the *Anvil Chorus* (from *Il Trovatore*) are heard as often in soccer stadiums or TV advertisements as they are in the opera house. Verdi's earliest surviving opera, *Oberto*, was a success. Then, just as suddenly, disaster struck. Verdi's next opera, *Un Giorno di Regno*, failed, and his two children and beloved wife died. In despair, he nearly gave up music. A friend from Italy's great opera house, La Scala, persuaded him to try again. His next opera, *Nabucco*, established his fame throughout Europe.

**ANTHEM FOR UNIFICATION**
In the early 1800s, Italy was a collection of states ruled by foreign powers. The political nature of Verdi's operas was in tune with Italy's nationalist feelings. When the King of Sardinia, Victor Emmanuel II, campaigned for a united Italy, the people's slogan became Viva VERDI—which stood for Vittorio Emanuele *Re D'Italia* (King of Italy).

| | |
|---|---|
| 1813 | *October 9, born in Le Roncole, near Busseto, Italy. His later music studies in Milan are sponsored by a local grocer.* |
| 1836 | *Marries his sponsor's daughter, Margherita Barezzi.* |
| 1838 | *Daughter dies.* |
| 1839 | *Second opera, Oberto, performed at La Scala, Milan. Wife and son die and he withdraws from music.* |
| 1842 | *Premieres third opera, Nabucco, in Milan; it is an international success.* |
| 1849 | *Becomes financially independent after writing an opera every year, and buys a farm at Sant' Agata.* |
| 1851 | *Rigoletto premieres in Venice, followed by Il Trovatore (1852) and La Traviata (1853).* |
| 1860 | *Italy is unified; Verdi is elected deputy in the first parliament.* |
| 1869 | *Soprano Giuseppina Strepponi becomes his second wife.* |
| 1871 | *Cairo premiere of Aïda celebrates the opening of the Suez Canal, which links the Mediterranean with the Indian Ocean.* |
| 1874 | *Composes Requiem in memory of Italian poet Alessandro Manzoni.* |
| 1884 | *Composer Arrigo Boito (1842–1918) provides librettos (stories) for his last operas, Otello (1887) and Falstaff (1892).* |
| 1901 | *January 27, dies in Milan. Buried beside his wife in the home he founded for retired musicians.* |

**FIRST SUCCESSES**
After Verdi's initial triumph, he began a period that lasted until 1855—his "galley" years, in which he slaved over many operas. It ended with three famous works: *Rigoletto*, a story about a hunchback, *Il Trovatore* (The Troubadour), and *La Traviata*, the story of a woman who falls in love, then dies of tuberculosis.

*La Traviata* costume design, 1935, by Konstantin Alekseevich

## "Verdi... has bursts of marvelous passion. His music at times exasperates, but it never bores."

**GEORGES BIZET (1818–75)**
French opera composer describing Verdi in a letter to a friend, 1859

**NABUCCO**
Verdi's big breakthrough came when his opera *Nabucco* opened to a run of 57 performances. This biblical story tells of the oppression of the Israelites in Babylon by King Nebuchadnezzar. The chorus sung by the Hebrew slaves—*Va, pensiero, sull'ali dorate* (Fly, thought, on wings of gold*)* was adopted as an anthem for Italy's political struggles.

Performance of *Nabucco* at La Scala, Milan, 1995

Fanfare trumpet, known
as an Aïda trumpet

*Three piston valves
control the notes
produced by the trumpet*

### INTERNATIONAL FAME

In 1870, Egypt celebrated the
opening of the Suez Canal. An opera
house was built in the city of Cairo and
Verdi wrote *Aïda*. The opera, set in ancient
Egypt, is about an Ethiopian slave girl in
love with Radames, the heroic captain of
the Egyptian Guard. Verdi's *Triumphal
March* plays as the army returns from battle,
accompanied on stage by slaves, horses,
camels, and sometimes elephants.

Pyramids and
Sphinx near
Cairo

*Arturo Toscanini
at Verdi's funeral*

### INSPIRED BY VERDI

Educated as a church
musician, Puccini heard
*Aïda* as a teenager. From
that moment on, he knew
he wanted to write opera.
Puccini is the greatest
heir to Verdi's legacy. His
superb orchestrations
and arias have made his
famous opera, *La Bohème,*
the box-office champion
at New York's Metropolitan
Opera. It has had
1,178 performances since
its Met debut in 1900.

Giacomo Puccini
(1858–1924)

### VERDI'S FUNERAL

As Verdi lay dying in a hotel in Milan,
straw was scattered on the cobbled
streets outside to muffle the sound of
passing carriages. At the funeral
service, the great Verdi
conductor, Toscanini, directed
a choir of over 800 singing
the slaves' chorus from
*Nabucco*. Over 250,000
followed the cortege.
Verdi was buried in
Milan in the chapel
of the *Casa Respori,*
his rest home for
poor musicians.
His epitaph is: "He
wept and loved for
everyone."

### FINAL ACT OF COMEDY

At the age of 80, when most composers
have retired, Verdi was at work on the
opera *Falstaff*. It was based on a play
by his favorite playwright, William
Shakespeare. Verdi had already
written the operas *Macbeth* and
*Otello* (Othello), which were
based on Shakespeare's
tragedies. But this one
was a comedy. Its hero,
Falstaff, is a fat,
cowardly rascal of
a knight from
Shakespeare's *Merry
Wives of Windsor.*

Bryn Terfel as *Sir John
Falstaff* at London's Royal
Opera House, 1999

**JOHANNES BRAHMS (1833–97)**
Brahms's works established him as a great composer alongside Bach and Beethoven—together, they are known as the "three Bs." Brahms was one of the first musicologists (musical historians) to revive Bach's music. He admired Beethoven, and a marble bust of the composer looked down on Brahms as he worked.

# Johannes Brahms

BRAHMS WAS THE LAST GREAT COMPOSER in the tradition of Beethoven. Although composing in the early Romantic era, he found everything he wanted in the Classical forms of the sonata, symphony, and concerto. Showing early promise on the piano, he helped to supplement the meager family income by playing the piano in restaurants and theatres. He was not a flashy performer like Liszt. Nor did he write dramatic operas or tone poems. This set him at odds with the more progressive composers of the day. Audiences in the 19th century took sides to either defend him or tear him down, like a great musical prize fighter.

**ANTONIO STRADIVARI**
The Stradivari family, from Cremona, Italy, made some of the greatest violins ever produced. The workshop was founded by Antonio (1644–1737) in 1680. A violinist is extremely lucky to ever get the chance to play one "Stradivarius," but Brahms's friend, the violinist Joseph Joachim, owned several. Few of the 700 instruments made still exist. One made in 1707 recently sold for $3 million.

| | |
|---|---|
| 1833 | *May 7, born in Hamburg, Germany, son of Johann Jakob Brahms, a double bassist.* |
| 1843 | *Starts piano lessons with Eduoard Marxsen (1806–87) and performs his first concert.* |
| 1853 | *His first performed work is* Piano Sonata in C Major. *Robert Schumann introduces him to violinist Joseph Joachim (1831–1907), and the two become friends.* |
| 1858 | *Completes* Piano Concerto in D minor. *It is premiered in 1859 in Hanover and Leipzig.* |
| 1868 | *Tours Germany, Austria, and Hungary with Joachim, then settles in Vienna, Austria. First performance of* Ein Deutsches Requiem (A German Requiem). |
| 1873 | *Finishes* Variations on a theme of Haydn (*the so-called* St. Antony Chorale); *writes versions for full orchestra and piano duo.* |
| 1878 | *Writes* Violin Concerto in D Major *and* Symphony No. 2. |
| 1883 | *Completes* Symphony No. 3 *and other works on a summer vacation.* |
| 1885 | *Rehearses* Symphony No. 4 *in Meningen, then tours Germany, the Netherlands, and, later, Italy.* |
| 1891 | *Writes* Clarinet Quintet *and the* Clarinet Trio. *Writes two more clarinet sonatas in 1894.* |
| 1896 | *Health deteriorates. April 1897, dies of cancer. He is buried in Vienna.* |

Robert and Clara Schumann

**LIFELONG FRIENDS**
Robert Schumann (1810–56) was one of the great Romantic composers (who wrote music based on literature that often tells a story). He was one of the first to spot Brahms's genius. His wife Clara (1819–96), a fine pianist and composer, was a huge influence on Brahms. When Robert became ill, Brahms helped them through his illness and death. Brahms and Clara remained very close for the rest of their lives.

### JOHANN STRAUSS THE YOUNGER

Brahms was lifelong friends with Strauss II (1825–99), who was known as Vienna's "Waltz King" when the city was the world's music center. Brahms is said to have remarked that he would have given anything to have written *The Blue Danube* waltz. It is said that he wrote "alas, not by Brahms!" on Strauss's score.

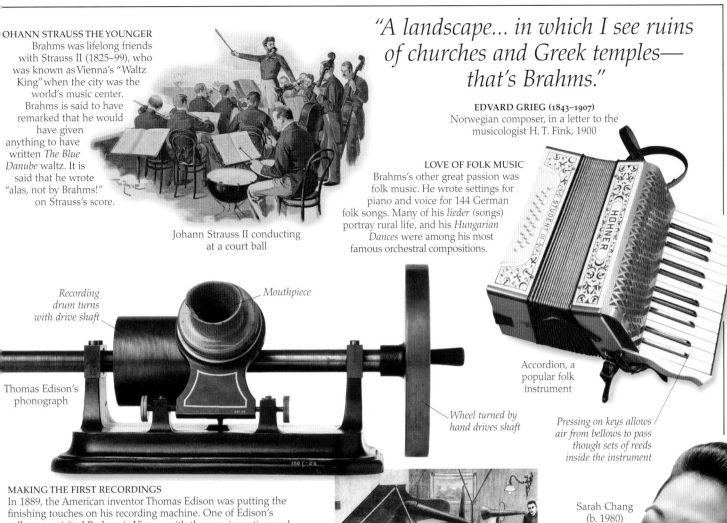

Johann Strauss II conducting at a court ball

## "A landscape... in which I see ruins of churches and Greek temples— that's Brahms."

**EDVARD GRIEG (1843–1907)**
Norwegian composer, in a letter to the musicologist H. T. Fink, 1900

### LOVE OF FOLK MUSIC

Brahms's other great passion was folk music. He wrote settings for piano and voice for 144 German folk songs. Many of his *lieder* (songs) portray rural life, and his *Hungarian Dances* were among his most famous orchestral compositions.

Accordion, a popular folk instrument

*Recording drum turns with drive shaft*

*Mouthpiece*

Thomas Edison's phonograph

*Wheel turned by hand drives shaft*

*Pressing on keys allows air from bellows to pass though sets of reeds inside the instrument*

### MAKING THE FIRST RECORDINGS

In 1889, the American inventor Thomas Edison was putting the finishing touches on his recording machine. One of Edison's colleagues visited Brahms in Vienna with the new invention and made one of the earliest recordings of Brahms playing part of his first *Hungarian Dance* on the piano. There is a bit of speaking at the beginning of the recording that is thought be Brahms's voice.

Phonograph in action

Sarah Chang (b. 1980)

### FAVORITE VIOLIN CONCERTO

Brahms composed works for chamber groups, but he wrote only one violin concerto—the *Violin Concerto in D*. The Korean American violinist Sarah Chang is one of many who perform it today. Its first soloist, Joseph Joachim, was one of the most influential violinists of all time. Joachim transcribed all of Brahms's *Hungarian Dances* for violin and piano.

### GERMAN REQUIEM

Brahms established his reputation as a composer in Vienna with the first performance of *A German Requiem,* a piece for choir, orchestra, and soloists. Although his mother and friend Robert Schumann had recently died, Brahms insisted it was written to comfort the living, not to remember the dead. Unusually, he wrote it in German, instead of Latin, so that people could understand it.

# Pyotr Ilyich Tchaikovsky

TCHAIKOVSKY'S MUSIC EXPERTLY BLENDS the European forms of the symphony, concerto, and opera with the vitality and flavor of his native Russian music. He is the most overtly emotional of all the Romantic composers: sometimes feverish and desperate, sometimes ecstatic with joy, other times hushed and secretive. His mother died when he was 14, and he suffered enormously during his life. His 1877 marriage was disastrous, and the effects of this nearly drove him mad. As a result, his music became his boldest public statement and his greatest private refuge. His tone poem *Romeo and Juliet* is an all-time favorite, and his concertos for violin and piano are essential for any soloist's repertoire. Tchaikovsky also wrote 11 operas, but most of all he is known for his three famous ballets, *Swan Lake, The Nutcracker,* and *Sleeping Beauty.*

**THE RUSSIAN FIVE**
In the mid-1800s, a group of Russian composers began to use folk music as their inspiration—an early expression of nationalism. Their leader was Mily Balakirev, and the other members were Modest Mussorgsky, Nicolai Rimsky-Korsakov, Alexander Borodin, and César Cui. The group is sometimes known as "The Mighty Handful."

**PYOTR ILYICH TCHAIKOVSKY (1840–93)**
Creator of some of the greatest melodies, Tchaikovsky is the most iconic of all Russian composers. He transformed a difficult personal life into great music. His many compositions form the pinnacle of 19th-century Russian music.

| | |
|---|---|
| 1840 | *May 7, born in Votkinsk, Russia.* |
| 1850 | *Begins composing. Sent to school in St. Petersburg.* |
| 1859 | *Enters the Ministry of Justice as a clerk. Resigns after four years to study music theory with Nicolai Zaremba (1821–79) and orchestration under Anton Rubinstein (1829–94).* |
| 1869 | *Begins* Romeo and Juliet *fantasy overture on a theme suggested by composer Mily Balakirev (1837–1910).* |
| 1874 | *Dedicates* Piano Concerto in B Flat Minor *to conductor Hans von Bülow (1830–94).* |
| 1876 | *Meets Franz Liszt. Begins correspondence with von Meck.* |
| 1877 | *Begins* Symphony No. 4. *and premieres* Swan Lake *in Moscow.* |
| 1879 | *Premieres best-known opera,* Eugene Onegin, *in Moscow.* |
| 1887 | *In St. Petersburg, makes first appearance as a conductor.* |
| 1888 | *Makes a European concert tour and meets many other composers, including Brahms, Grieg, and Dvořák.* |
| 1891 | *Visits US. Conducts at opening of New York's Carnegie Hall.* |
| 1893 | *Begins* Symphony No. 6, the Pathétique. *Receives honorary degree from England's Cambridge University. Back in St. Petersburg, conducts his sixth symphony, develops cholera, and dies.* |

Letter to Madame von Meck
from Germany, 1889

**ECCENTRIC PATRON**
One of the more extraordinary features of Tchaikovsky's life was his 13-year correspondence with a wealthy widow, Nadezhda von Meck. She gave him an annuity (annual salary) and they wrote to each other, but they agreed never to meet. She was a fanatical lover of Tchaikovsky's music and acted as his agony aunt. He dedicated his sweeping *Fourth Symphony* to "my best friend."

*"I am Russian in the completest possible sense of that word."*

**TCHAIKOVSKY**
writing to Madame von Meck, 1878

**DANCE OF THE SWANS**
The Russian Imperial Ballet reached its artistic summit with the ballets of Tchaikovsky. The first, *Swan Lake,* premiered in 1877. It is a magical story about a princess turned into a swan by an evil sorcerer. Tchaikovsky's ballets stood as a model that attracted composers such as Stravinsky and Sergei Prokofiev.

## CONCERT CLASSIC

Tchaikovsky's *1812 Overture* was written for Moscow's Arts and Industry Exhibition in 1881. The title recalls the year the Russian army successfully stood against Napoleon's French army. The music conjures up the opposing armies with Russian folk songs and the French anthem, *La Marseillaise,* and the finale has real cannons. Oddly, Tchaikovsky later said, "I'm undecided as to whether my overture is good or bad, but it is probably the latter."

THE
GUILDHALL EDITION.
Continental Fingering
Nº 33.

# TCHAIKOWSKY.

# 1812
# OVERTURE
## OP.49.

## THE NUTCRACKER

This Christmas classic ballet is based on a story by E. T. A. Hoffman called the *Nutcracker and the Mouse King,* in which a present— a nutcracker—comes to life as a prince. It premiered in St. Petersburg's Mariinsky Theater in 1891. Tchaikovsky was the first composer to use a celeste, a keyboard that plays bells. He used the sound to characterize the central figure, the Sugar Plum Fairy.

Nutcracker in the form of a painted toy soldier

Russian cannon used in Napoleonic Wars

Dancers from Moscow's Bolshoi Ballet company performing *Swan Lake,* 2004

## VALERY GERGIEV

Under the leadership of this outstanding Russian conductor (b. 1953), St. Petersburg's Mariinsky Theater (called the Kirov in the Soviet era) has been transformed into a powerhouse of opera and ballet. His performances of Tchaikovsky's works have set a world standard. "A lot of people," reflects Gergiev, "struggle to find what they identify with. I am very lucky. I crossed the piazza just once in St. Petersburg, from the Music Conservatory to the door of the Mariinsky. That was the only important journey of my life."

# Antonín Dvořák

**ANTONÍN DVOŘÁK (1841–1904)**
Inspired by the legends and music of his native Bohemia, Dvořák wrote many tone poems (short orchestral stories) that vividly portray goblins and other mythical creatures. His music is as memorable as a folk song, but as sophisticated as any composer's.

"I AM JUST AN ORDINARY CZECH MUSICIAN" was Dvořák's opinion of himself. He was certainly born in humble circumstances in a country village. Both his father and his grandfather were butchers, but they also played the zither, a harplike folk instrument. Dvořák drew much of his inspiration from folk music, writing exhilarating pieces for just about every kind of performance, from solo piano to orchestral and chamber music. His music is remarkable for its spontaneity and rhythm—his *Slavonic Dances* are favorites of orchestras and audiences alike. His early successes drew the attention of composer Johannes Brahms, who remained one of his greatest admirers. After achieving fame in Europe, Dvořák was invited to New York as director of the new National Conservatory of Music. He accepted, and composed some of his greatest works during his stay.

| | |
|---|---|
| 1841 | September 8, born in the village of Nelahozeves, Bohemia, now in the Czech Republic. |
| c.1857 | Sent to the Prague Organ School, where he studies violin and viola. |
| 1866 | Joins Bohemian Provincial Theater Orchestra as viola player. |
| 1873 | Marries Anna Cernakova, a sister of one his pupils. First performs the cantata (choir piece) Hymnus. |
| 1875 | Wins Ministry of Education Grant for composition, and again a couple of years later. Brahms is on the selection panel both times and recommends Dvořák to his publisher, Fritz Simrock. |
| 1877 | Writes Stabat Mater ("Sorrowful Mother is Standing"), a setting of a Roman Catholic prayer about Jesus' mother by his cross. |
| 1878 | Composes and publishes Slavonic Dance, Book One. |
| 1883 | Is invited to England and performs a series of concerts. |
| 1892 | Moves to New York and becomes director of the National Conservatory of Music. |
| 1893 | Premieres his ninth symphony, From the New World. |
| 1901 | Returns to Prague and becomes director of the Conservatory. Gives first performance of his opera Rusalka there. |
| 1904 | Dies. His death is mourned with a national funeral, and he is buried in Prague. |

**AMERICAN FAMILY VACATION**
During his years in the US, Dvořák (pictured here with his family just after their arrival) worked very hard. He missed his native Bohemia, so the family traveled for four days to visit a Czechoslovakian community—Spillville, Iowa.

**BOHEMIAN FOLK MUSIC**
Written for two pianos, Dvořák's *Slavonic Dances* were an early success based on national folk music. Bohemian fairy tales also inspired his exquisite orchestral tone poems, such as *The Noonday Witch* and *The Golden Spinning Wheel*. Dvořák's most popular opera, *Rusalka*, is a based on a tale of a water-nymph who falls in love with a prince.

Traditional Bohemian folk-dancer's costume

French-born American cellist Yo Yo Ma (b. 1955)

**CELLO CONCERTO**
Dvořák's *Cello Concerto* remains the most performed and recorded concerto for the instrument. As a viola player and violinist, Dvořák knew just how to create rewarding pieces for string instruments. He also composed 14 string quartets. The most famous of these, the *American Quartet*, was written while on vacation in Spillville.

### AFRICAN-AMERICAN MUSIC
Dvořák was fascinated by the music of African Americans. He and was introduced to them by Harry T. Burleigh, a gifted singer and energetic collector of Negro spirituals. Dvořák wrote that in these melodies, "I discover all that is needed for a great and noble school of music. They are pathetic, tender, passionate, melancholy, solemn, religious, bold, merry, happy, or what you will."

Harry T. Burleigh (1866–1949)

### FROM AMERICA TO THE MOON
Dvořák's final symphony, his ninth, is his most popular. It features in a slow, second movement a serene melody influenced by American folk music. Dvořák said that its title, *From the New World,* only signified "Impressions and greetings from the New World" where he was now living. America loved the work. In 1969, Neil Armstrong took a recording on the *Apollo* space mission when he was in search of a new world—the Moon.

Buzz Aldrin photographed by Neil Armstrong on the first ever moonwalk

> "I should be glad if something occurred to me as a main idea that occurs to Dvořák only by the way."

**JOHANNES BRAHMS**
writing about Dvořák, the musician he supported and admired

### EDVARD GRIEG
Like Dvořák, Grieg (1843–1907) loved his native country. This Norwegian's pieces are popular all around the world. They include his piano concerto and music for Ibsen's play *Peer Gynt.* His *In the Hall of the Mountain King* and *Morning Mood* are often recorded, and even feature in Warner Bros. *Looney Tunes* cartoons.

Spectacular Scandinavian fjord

Sibelius on cover of *Time* magazine, 1937

### JEAN SIBELIUS
Finnish composer Sibelius (1865–1957) was another inspired by his country's landscape, folklore, and music. The lakes and forests of Finland fired his imagination, and he conveyed this through his ruggedly individual music. Many of his works are based on an ancient Finnish epic, the *Kalevala.* He wrote seven symphonies and a popular violin concerto.

# Richard Strauss

**RICHARD STRAUSS (1864–1949)**
Not since Mozart had there been a composer who so expertly created drama by setting words to music. Strauss was one of the greatest composers for singers, from his earliest works to *The Four Last Songs* (1948), his final masterpiece.

STRAUSS WAS A GENIUS AT MUSICAL storytelling. His first successes came with his tone poems—pieces of music for orchestra that tell a story. And what stories they were: the dashing *Don Juan*, the mischievous *Till Eulenspiegel* (a German folk hero), and the epic *Ein Heldenleben* (*A Hero's Life*), in which Strauss portrays himself as the hero and music critics as his enemies. Although the tone poems established Strauss's name as a young composer, his operas are his crowning glory. After his very first operas failed, he returned with the scandalous success *Salome*, which was based on the New Testament story of Herod's daughter and her love for John the Baptist, as told by the playwright Oscar Wilde. Strauss followed this with a drama of family revenge, *Elektra*, based on a Greek tragedy, in which the shocking plot is matched by the feverish orchestration. In all, Strauss wrote 15 operas.

| | |
|---|---|
| 1864 | *June 11, born in Munich, Germany. His father, a French-horn player with the Court Orchestra, teaches him from an early age.* |
| 1881 | *Writes* Symphony No. 1. *His* String Quartet *is performed in Munich.* |
| 1882 | *Enrolls at Munich University (to study art history and philosophy).* |
| 1885 | *Becomes assistant conductor to Hans von Bülow in Meiningen.* |
| 1889 | *Becomes staff conductor at the opera house in Weimar.* |
| 1890s | *Tone poems such as Don Juan establish him as a composer.* |
| 1894 | *Marries soprano Pauline de Ahna, who was famously bossy.* |
| 1905 | *Premieres* Salome *in Dresden, and shocks audiences.* |
| 1909 | *Premiere of* Elektra *begins partnership with librettist Hugo von Hoffmannsthal (1874–1929).* |
| 1901 | *Composes opera* Der Rosenkavalier. |
| 1933 | *Appointed director of the Nazi Reichsmusikkammer (Music Bureau), but is forced to resign in 1935.* |
| 1945 | *Leaves Germany with his wife and travels to Switzerland.* |
| 1947 | *Visits London and conducts his own works.* |
| 1949 | *Dies at his villa near Garmisch.* |

### ARIADNE AUF NAXOS

Written with von Hoffmannsthal, this opera was first performed on 1912. It tells the story of the richest man in Vienna, who wants to entertain guests to a play and an opera based on a Greek myth. As the two groups of artistes prepare, he tells them to perform both at the same time. The opera part shows a sad Ariadne abandoned on the island of Naxos. The play's actors attempt to cheer her up just as the god of wine, Bacchus, arrives to rescue her.

*Jeanne Piland as Feldmarschallin*

*Annette Seiltgen in the role of Octavia, dressed as a boy*

Welsh National Opera's 2004 production of *Ariadne auf Naxos*

### COMIC TRIUMPH

Strauss said he found putting von Hoffmannsthal's words to music "as easy as spreading butter." The pair set their second opera, *Der Rosenkavalier* (*The Knight of the Rose*), in the home of an 18th-century princess. The comic treatment of the tangled love story of the main characters is brilliant. Memorable, too, are the score's famous waltzes. However, this German Strauss is not related to Vienna's "Waltz King," Johann Strauss II.

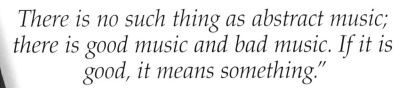

*There is no such thing as abstract music; there is good music and bad music. If it is good, it means something."*

**RICHARD STRAUSS**
describing 20th-century music

## CONTROVERSIAL NAZI CONNECTIONS
The German Nazi Party was stridently anti-Semitic and tried to eliminate any trace of Jewish culture. In 1933, without consulting Strauss, the Nazis appointed him president of the *Reichsmusikkammer*, the State Music Bureau. Strauss accepted, perhaps to help protect his Jewish daughter-in-law, Alice.

Commemorative badge for 1936 Olympics

## MOUNTAIN HOME
In 1908, Strauss built a villa near Garmisch, high in the German Alps, as his summer house. His daughter-in-law was held here under house arrest in 1938. During World War II, Strauss relocated to Austria and followed the progress of the war and the destruction of his beloved Germany from Vienna. His great sadness is reflected in *Metamorphosen* (1945), a piece written for a small string orchestra. After moving to Switzerland, he returned to Garmisch in 1949, but died soon after.

## BERLIN OLYMPIC GAMES
In 1935, Strauss had to resign as president of the Music Bureau, because his librettist and friend, Stefan Zweig, was Jewish. Strauss had written Zweig a supportive letter, which was intercepted by the Nazi secret police, the Gestapo. In 1932 Strauss had been asked to write the Olympic Hymn for the opening of the 1936 Olympics. He conducted its premiere at the games, but did not think much of it.

Performance by the Singapore Symphony Orchestra

## THE LANGUAGE OF FILM
Movies have always depended on music to help tell their story, and Strauss's lush, romantic style influenced many film composers. One of the greatest was Erich Wolfgang Korngold (1897–1957). An Austro-Hungarian, Korngold was a child prodigy. He moved to the US in World War II. He wrote the music for movies such as the swashbuckling *Adventures of Robin Hood*.

## MODERN ORCHESTRAL SOUND
Strauss became the conductor of the Meiningen Orchestra at the age of 21, and later of the Munich Opera. These jobs allowed him to hear a large orchestra with over 100 musicians play day in and day out. Through this he developed an understanding of the impact that the sound of big orchestra can have. Using this knowledge, he perfected his compositions and created the clear sound of the modern orchestra.

Poster for the 1938 movie *Robin Hood*, starring Errol Flynn and Olivia de Havilland

## KUBRICK'S 2001: A SPACE ODYSSEY
Strauss's *Also Sprach Zarathustra* (*Thus Spoke Zarathustra*) was inspired by the poetry of German philosopher Friedrich Nietzsche. Nietzsche wrote of humanity's potential as a race of superior beings, and Strauss's music depicts human progress from simple hunter to masters of the world. The music was used in the movie *2001: A Space Odyssey* by Stanley Kubrick, which tells the story as science fiction.

# Igor Stravinsky

**IGOR STRAVINSKY (1882–1971)**
Stravinsky was Russian by birth but cosmopolitan by nature. He lived in several continents, eras, and cultures, finally settling in the US. An iconic figure, he was voted among the 100 most influential people of the 20th century by *Time* magazine in 1999.

AT THE AGE OF NINE, Stravinsky was first mesmerized by the sound of the Russian Imperial Opera's orchestra performing Tchaikovsky's *Sleeping Beauty*. He grew up with the colorful sound of Russian folk music, which he wove with shimmering virtuosity into his early works. Although a talented musician as a boy, he studied law to please his parents. Later he switched to music and laid the foundations for what became some of the most original and influential music of the 20th century. His music sometimes borrows from folk melodies, sometimes from the classics, but Stravinsky's startling rhythms and bewitching harmonies make his music instantly recognizable.

**RIMSKY-KORSAKOV**
Stravinsky's most important teacher, Rimsky-Korsakov (1844–1908) was a successful composer whose colorful music paved the way for Stravinsky's groundbreaking orchestral pieces. He was a member of the group called The Mighty Handful (see p30), which championed music with a strong Russian character.

| | |
|---|---|
| 1882 | *July 17, born near St. Petersburg, Russia. Father is principal bass singer at the Mariinsky Theater.* |
| 1902 | *Enrolls at St. Petersburg University to study law. Also studies composition with family friend Rimsky-Korsakov.* |
| 1906 | *Marries his cousin Katerina Nossenko.* |
| 1909 | *Diaghilev commissions* The Firebird *for Ballets Russes.* |
| 1910 | *French composer Claude Debussy (1862–1918) admires his work; he and Stravinsky become friends.* |
| 1913 | *Le Sacre du Printemps (The Rite of Spring) premieres in Paris.* |
| 1920 | *Moves to France with his family.* |
| 1928 | *Apollo premieres in the US with choreography by George Balanchine.* |
| 1939 | *Moves to the US after the deaths of his eldest daughter and wife.* |
| 1940 | *Marries again. The Rite of Spring is used in Walt Disney's* Fantasia. |
| 1945 | *Jazz experiments result in the Ebony Concerto written for clarinetist Woody Herman.* |
| 1951 | *Premieres his opera The Rake's Progress in Venice.* |
| 1962 | *Visits Russia for the first time in over 40 years. President John F. Kennedy is assassinated— Stravinsky composes his Elegy.* |
| 1971 | *Stravinsky dies in New York. He is buried in Venice, near Diaghilev.* |

**BALLET WITH BALANCHINE**
George Balanchine (1904–83), a fellow Russian, first met Stravinsky when he choreographed his ballet *Apollo* for the Ballets Russes in 1928. They continued their partnership in America with Balanchine's new company, the New York City Ballet. Over the course of 40 years, Balanchine created more than 30 ballets using Stravinsky's music. Stravinsky said that seeing Balanchine choreograph his music was "like a tour of a building for which I had drawn the plans but never explored."

Vaslav Nijinsky, lead dancer with the Ballet Russes, performing *Petrushka*

**DIAGHILEV'S BALLETS RUSSES**
Stravinsky's most significant early collaborator was Serge Diaghilev (1872–1929), the flamboyant founder of the Ballets Russes (Russian Ballet). Their first success was *The Firebird,* based on a Russian folk tale about a demon who has 13 princesses under his spell. This was followed by *Petrushka,* about a puppet that comes to life. Both featured the exotic costumes and sets that were a hallmark of the Ballets Russes.

## BENNY GOODMAN

American swing-jazz clarinetist Benny Goodman (1909–86) was also an expert classical musician. He worked with many composers, including Leonard Bernstein, and was just at home with a an orchestra as with a jazz band. Stravinsky's fascination with jazz led him to write the bluesy *Ebony Concerto*, which Goodman performed and recorded with him.

*Ebony is the wood used to make clarinets*

Clarinet

## LEOPOLD STOKOWSKI

One of the most glamorous conductors of the 20th century, Leopold Stokowski (1882–1977) championed Stravinsky's music. "Stoki" appeared in Walt Disney's movie *Fantasia* alongside Mickey Mouse. He conducted the excerpt of Stravinsky's *The Rite of Spring* that accompanied the sequence showing the beginning of prehistoric life, the dinosaurs, and their eventual destruction.

## *"My music is best understood by children and animals."*

**STRAVINSKY**
in London's *Observer* newspaper, October 1961

*Tamara Rojo in the leading role*

## THE RITE OF SPRING

The 1913 premiere of this ballet at the Théâtre des Champs-Élysées in Paris by the Ballets Russes created a scandal. The angular, primitive choreography showing a pagan girl dancing herself to death was as shocking as the music's pounding rhythms and dissonant chords. Soon the agitated audience began to boo the "barbaric" ballet. This was the beginning of modern music, and it established Stravinsky's worldwide fame.

London's Royal Ballet performing *The Rite of Spring,* at the Royal Opera House, 2005

Portrait by Richard Gerstl

**ARNOLD SCHOENBERG (1874–1951)**
Schoenberg followed in the footsteps of Bach, Beethoven, and Brahms as an innovative German composer. Much of his music does not sound anything like the work of these composers, until you listen closer. He was also an avid tennis player and had a terrible fear of the number 13.

| | |
|---|---|
| 1874 | *September 13, born in the Jewish quarter of Vienna, Austria.* |
| 1890 | *Becomes a bank clerk to support his widowed mother and studies music in the evenings.* |
| 1899 | *Writes* Verklärte Nacht *(Transfigured Night), a work for string sextet (six players).* |
| 1901 | *Marries Mathilde, sister of his friend and teacher, Alexander von Zemlinsky (1871–1942).* |
| 1903 | *Becomes composition teacher at Stern Conservatory in Berlin.* |
| 1912 | *Premieres revolutionary* Pierrot Lunaire; *it is a huge success.* |
| 1913 | *In Vienna, premieres* Gurrelieder, *the work that sums up his most romantic musical language.* |
| 1916 | *Joins the Austrian army, but is discharged in 1917 for being sickly.* |
| 1918 | *Founds Society for Private Musical Performances to help promote his new music.* |
| 1924 | *His first wife dies and he marries Gertrud Kolisch.* |
| 1925 | *Appointed professor at the Berlin Academy of Arts.* |
| 1933 | *Leaves Germany for US because of anti-Jewish Nazi regime. Becomes a US citizen in 1941.* |
| 1948 | *World premiere of* Survivor from Warsaw. |
| 1951 | *Friday, July 13 (at 13 minutes to midnight), dies in Los Angeles.* |

# Arnold Schoenberg

ONE OF AUSTRIA'S MAJOR composers, Arnold Schoenberg started out as a self-taught, post-Romantic musician. He became fascinated by atonal music (music without traditional harmony). He even invented a system of composing using all twelve pitches of a scale, outlined in his *Book of Hanging Gardens* (1908). You would not expect this from listening to his early works. His *Transfigured Night* (1899) is one of the most evocative pieces ever written. Schoenberg's major work, *Gurrelieder*, performed by a huge orchestra, four choirs, five soloists, and a speaker, was composed in the pioneering mold of his peers, Richard Strauss and Gustav Mahler (1860–1911). Schoenberg's work has inspired more controversy than any other 20th-century composer.

*The Kiss* by Gustav Klimt, 1907–8

**CONTEMPORARY ART**
Schoenberg was very aware of Vienna's heritage. As an amateur painter, his compositions were also influenced by the work of contemporary Viennese painters. One group, the Expressionists, included Vassily Kandinsky. They used vivid colors to express emotions in their paintings. Another group interested in sensual ways of looking at the world included Gustav Klimt. Schoenberg used both approaches in his music.

**PIERROT LUNAIRE**
This dreamlike masterpiece is a series of songs based on the poems of French poet Albert Giraud (1860–1929). The eerie music was written using an early version of Schoenberg's atonal system. The music fits perfectly with the image of the strange clown, Pierrot, who sings in the moonlight in a weird half-spoken, half-sung voice.

Sally Burgess singing *Pierrot Lunaire* at London's Almeida Theatre, 2006

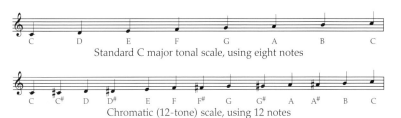

Standard C major tonal scale, using eight notes

C    D    E    F    G    A    B    C

Chromatic (12-tone) scale, using 12 notes

C C# D D# E F F# G G# A A# B C

## LIFE IN HOLLYWOOD

Many European immigrants arrived in the US in the 1930s. Some moved to Los Angeles in search of work. Schoenberg taught at the University of California and became friends with several celebrities, including George Gershwin. Gershwin was a great fan of Schoenberg and painted his portrait as a tribute. They were both fanatical tennis players and often played tennis together.

Gershwin painting Schoenberg, December 1936

## ALL NOTES ARE EQUAL

Western music is arranged in groups of eight notes (octaves). When, for example, as C major scale is played on a piano, there are eight notes (the white keys). Some of these notes are especially important within the scale and contribute to tonal harmony. Schoenberg invented a way of composing that was not confined by these harmonies, and used all twelve notes (the white and black keys) in the octave, treating them equally. Schoenberg wrote all kinds of music with this technique.

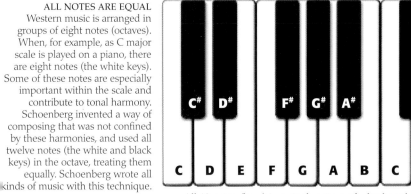

All 12 notes (keys) in a single octave of a keyboard

## "My music is not modern, it is only badly played"

**SCHOENBERG**
describing his work, from *Schoenberg*, by Charles Rosen, published 1976

## BIBLICAL OPERA

Schoenberg based his unfinished opera *Moses und Aron* on the Old Testament story in which God reveals his laws to Moses, and Moses in turn passes them to the Israelites through his brother Aaron. (Schoenberg changed the spelling of Aaron so there would not be 13 letters in the title.) Schoenberg converted to Protestantism in 1898, but anti-Semitism in the 1930s prompted him to return to Judaism.

Cover for 1996 recording conducted by Pierre Boulez

## JEWISH SETTLERS

Schoenberg was one of millions of Jews who fled Europe because of religious persecution. He wrote a dramatic work called *A Survivor from Warsaw*, which focused on this experience. It relates how a group of Jews from the Warsaw Ghetto (an area in which the Nazis forced Jews to live) who are about to be killed, suddenly burst into song. They sing the *Sh'ma*, the prayer that embodies the Jewish religion and says, "O Israel, the Lord is our God."

Star of David with the German word for Jew

Yellow badge that the Nazis forced Jews to wear

Shoenberg's memorial in the Central Cemetery in Vienna

## MONUMENTAL MUSIC

Schoenberg's life was a struggle, and he spent most of it as an outsider. Misunderstood by the establishment, his music was denied the glory that it would win for him after his death. However, he was honored with a burial in the Central Cemetery in Vienna, along with notable composers such as Brahms, Beethoven, and Johann Strauss II.

# George Gershwin

**GEORGE GERSHWIN (1898–1937)**
Gershwin did not fit the mold of a serious composer. For one thing all of his precedessors were European. Gershwin felt this when met his Austrian idol Alban Berg (1885–1935) in Vienna in 1928. However, Berg put him at ease when he said "But Mr. Gershwin, music is music."

No ONE MADE AS GREAT an impact on the American popular song (pop song) as George Gershwin, but he led a double musical life, making his mark as a classical composer as well. He was born Jacob Gershowitz into a Jewish immigrant family who had arrived in the US in the late 1800s. Gershwin's first published song, *When You Want 'Em, You Can't Get 'Em*, only earned him five dollars. Soon afterward, in 1919, he composed *Swanee*, which was made famous by the singer Al Jolson (1886–1950) and sold over a million copies. His older brother Ira was already busy writing lyrics for other songwriters. In 1924, the brothers collaborated on their first musical, *Lady Be Good.* It was the start of a lasting and successful partnership.

*Statue of Liberty, New York*

**THE MEN WHO MADE AMERICA SING**
Millions of Jewish immigrants looked for a new life in America. The Gershwins found themselves in New York among families who also fled persecution in Eastern Europe and Russia. Other great musicians from similar backgrounds were Irving Berlin (Israel Isidore Baline), Jerome Kern, and Al Jolson (Asa Yoelson).

| | |
|---|---|
| **1898** | *September 26, born in Brooklyn, New York, son of Russian Jewish immigrants. He is the second of four children—Ira, George, Arthur, and Frances.* |
| **1910** | *Starts to study piano.* |
| **1914** | *Takes a job as pianist for music publishers Jerome Remick & Co.* |
| **1918** | *George and Ira Gershwin write their first song together,* The Real American Folk Song. |
| **1924** | *Premieres his first big orchestral success,* Rhapsody in Blue, *with Paul Whiteman's band at the Aeolian Hall, New York. Musical* Lady Be Good *opens.* |
| **1925** | *Premieres another classical piece,* Piano Concerto in F. |
| **1928** | *New York Philharmonic Orchestra premieres musical* An American in Paris. *He travels to Europe and meets composers Maurice Ravel, Alban Berg, and Sergei Prokofiev.* |
| **1930** | *Girl Crazy opens on Broadway, starring Ginger Rogers and Ethel Merman.* |
| **1931** | *Of Thee I Sing opens and is awarded the Pulitzer Prize for Drama the following year.* |
| **1935** | *Opera* Porgy and Bess *premieres at the Alvine Theater in New York.* |
| **1937** | *Dies of a brain tumor in Los Angeles without leaving a will, so his mother inherits his fortune.* |
| **1998** | *Awarded a posthumous Pulitzer prize for his work.* |

*"George's music gets around so much before an opening that the first-night audience thinks it's at a revival."*

**GEORGE S. KAUFMAN (1889–1961)**
American playwright, theater director, and drama critic

**NEW YORK'S TIN PAN ALLEY**
Gershwin began his musical career as a publisher's song-plugger. In the days before CDs and tapes, "pluggers" would play new songs to music publishers in the hope of selling them on. The area where the publishers had their offices—West 28th Street between Broadway and Sixth Avenue—became known as "Tin Pan Alley," because all the pianos playing at the same time sounded like clashing tin pans.

*Clarke Peters performs the role of Porgy*

Production of *Porgy and Bess* at London's Savoy Theatre, 2006

## RHAPSODY IN BLUE

In 1924, Paul Whiteman and his band wanted a jazzy piano concerto for a concert called *An Experiment in Modern Music*, which mixed classics with new works. Although working on a show, Gershwin was eager to write for the concert hall. He hurriedly sketched a piece on a train journey to Boston. Called *Rhapsody in Blue*, this became Gershwin's most famous classical piece.

Paul Whiteman's band performs *Rhapsody in Blue* in the 1930 movie *King of Jazz*

Car horns used in the movie *An American in Paris*

## HOLLYWOOD CONNECTIONS

Gershwin wrote a tone poem (musical story) evoking the sights and sounds that an American tourist sees on a visit to the French capital. Called *An American in Paris*, it was written for an orchestra, but Gershwin couldn't resist adding a set of authentic Parisian taxi horns—the effect was stunning. The piece was made into a movie starring Gene Kelly.

## THE FAMILY ACT

The lion's share of Gershwin's musical hits were written with his brother, Ira. Together they wrote over two dozen shows for New York's Broadway theaters—many were also made into movies. The shows featured the songs that form the bedrock of the *Great American Songbook*. Ira reached the top of his profession in 1932 as the first lyricist to win a Pulitzer Prize for their show, *Of Thee I Sing*.

Poster for 1927 production of *Funny Face*, starring Fred and Adele Astaire

*Maurice Ravel at the piano*

*George Gershwin*

*Canadian singer Éva Gauthier*

## MAURICE RAVEL

Gershwin was greatly influenced by the French composer Maurice Ravel (1875–1937). He loved Ravel's music and his piano playing. Gershwin heard in Ravel's music a very refined and magical treatment of the modern and jazzy harmonies that he used himself.

*Nicola Hughes as the heroine Bess*

## PORGY AND BESS

The summit of Gershwin's musical ambition was reached in his folk opera, *Porgy and Bess*. No other opera has managed to combine popular music, blues, and jazz with grand opera. The result was famous songs like *Summertime* and *I Got Plenty o' Nuttin'*. In addition, *Porgy and Bess* was the first opera that required a cast of classically trained African-American singers. The 1935 production starred Tod Duncan and Ann Brown.

# Duke Ellington

**EDWARD KENNEDY ELLINGTON (1899–1974)**
His golden touch as a composer was matched by his sophistication and charm. As a boy, his friends noticed that his casual, off-hand manner, his easy grace, and his smart dress gave him the bearing of a young nobleman, so they called him Duke.

THE MOST SOPHISTICATED and influential figure in American jazz, Ellington was largely responsible for elevating jazz from simply entertainment to a unique form of artistic expression. He was a pianist, band leader, and composer whose imagination knew no bounds. His music was influenced by ragtime and Dixie music from the South. He wrote songs, ballets, musicals, and groundbreaking film scores. His legendary band toured the globe, playing in roadside clubs and major concert halls. He drew inspiration from many sources, including William Shakespeare (listen to *Such Sweet Thunder*) and Tchaikovsky, whose *Nutcracker Suite* he arranged for his band. Ellington's songs were unforgettable tunes, swinging dance numbers, and showcases for his soloists. His greatest hit became his motto: "It Don't Mean a Thing If It Ain't Got That Swing."

**AVID SPORTSMAN**
The young Ellington was more interested in track and baseball than music. His first job was selling peanuts at Washington Senators baseball games. He studied art, only taking up music seriously in his late teens

| | |
|---|---|
| 1899 | *April 29, born in Washington DC, to Daisy and James Ellington, both amateur pianists. His father is a part-time butler at the White House.* |
| 1906 | *Begins piano lessons with Mrs. Clinkscales (true), but fails to show much interest.* |
| 1912 | *Writes his first composition, "Soda Fountain Rag," while working at the Poodle Dog Café. Soon after, he begins to take the piano seriously.* |
| 1916 | *Drops out of Armstrong Manual Training School, Washington, DC, where he studied commercial art, and declines scholarship to Pratt Institute of Fine Art in Brooklyn.* |
| 1918 | *Forms his first band, The Duke's Serenaders.* |
| 1923 | *Moves to Harlem, New York, and makes his first recording.* |
| 1927 | *Begins his five-year engagement at New York's Cotton Club.* |
| 1933 | *Makes his first tour to Europe; visits London and Paris.* |
| 1938 | *Arranger Billy Strayhorn joins Ellington's band.* |
| 1943 | *Makes his debut at Carnegie Hall, New York.* |
| 1959 | *Composes his first film soundtrack— the first by a black composer— Anatomy of a Murder.* |
| 1973 | *Publishes his autobiography, Music Is My Mistress.* |
| 1974 | *Dies of lung cancer at the age of 75.* |

**JAZZ CLUB GREATS**
There were many jazz clubs in 1920s New York. The legendary Cotton Club in Harlem, in the heart of the black community, was run by gangsters. It entertained a chic white clientele but featured prominent black artists. Ellington was a resident musician there and recorded over 100 compositions, built the foundations of the band he led for 50 years, and took on his writing partner, Billy Strayhorn.

**THE BIG BAND**
Ellington was a genius at writing music that made the most of his band's talents. The growling trumpets, swooning saxophones, and thundering jungle rhythms of the drums were colorful features of the "Ellington" sound. The musicians all knew each other so well from playing together over the years that it's hard to know where Ellington's compositions end and the band's interpretations begin.

President Nixon awarding the Medal of Freedom in 1970

Sheet music for *Take the "A" Train*, 1941

## BILLY STRAYHORN

Few musicians left a greater mark on the Ellington Band's sound than Billy "Sweet Pea" Strayhorn (1915–67). Ellington met the shy young arranger in Pittsburg, and asked him to come to New York. The result was a close 30-year collaboration. Strayhorn's early song, *Take the "A" Train* (the best way to get to Ellington's house in Harlem from Manhattan) became the band's theme song.

1930s radio

## AWARD WINNER

Ellington won many awards for his music. He also acted as an informal American ambassador of music on his many world tours. For this and his enormous contribution to music, he was honored by two US presidents. Lyndon B. Johnson gave him the Presidential Gold Medal in 1966. In his 70th birthday year, the Duke received one of the highest civilian honors in the US—the Presidential Medal of Freedom—from Richard Nixon.

Presidential Medal of Freedom

## EFFECT OF RADIO

Before the days of television, people heard the news, drama, soap operas, and all kinds of music on the radio. Music was usually performed live, whether jazz from a club or Arturo Toscanini conducting an orchestra. The weekly radio broadcasts from Harlem's Cotton Club were the Duke's launchpad to stardom.

*"Art is dangerous. It is one of the attractions: when it ceases to be dangerous you don't want it."*

**ELLINGTON**
in his autobiography, *Music Is My Mistress*, published 1973

## ELLA FITZGERALD

As a young girl in Virginia, Ella Fitzgerald (1917–96) fell in love with jazz and jazz singers. After a chaotic childhood she became a singer in a touring big band. It was with this band, imitating the saxophone and trumpet soloists, that she developed her fabulous vocal technique. She recorded the *Duke Ellington Songbook*, an addition to her landmark series *The Great American Songbook*. She became known as the "First Lady of Song."

# Richard Rodgers

AMERICA GAVE THE WORLD many musical gifts in the 20th century: among them the popular song and the musical (a theater production that integrates music, songs, speaking, and dance). No other composer produced as many works in both fields as Richard Rodgers. He transformed what began as a collection of catchy "Tin Pan Alley" songs strung together with jokes and dances into an integrated art form. He wrote over 900 songs and 40 musicals, performed in New York's Broadway theaters and London's West End, and received Pulitzer, Tony, Oscar, Emmy, and Grammy awards. His success was in contrast to his beginning—after years of struggle, he was about to take a job in an underwear store when he and Lorenz Hart had their first hit.

**RICHARD RODGERS (1902–79)**
The shows created by Richard Rodgers define American musical theater. He worked with many people, but he had two major collaborators: Lorenz (Larry) Hart (1895–1943), who was chaotic, but charmig, and Oscar Hammerstein II (1895–1960), who helped Rodgers create his greatest works.

| | |
|---|---|
| 1902 | *June 28, born in Long Island, New York, to a prosperous family.* |
| 1919 | *Meets Lorenz Hart through his brother's friends at Columbia University.* |
| 1921 | *Attends the Institute of Musical Art, New York.* |
| 1925 | *With Hart, writes their breakthrough song, "Manhattan," as part of* The Garrick Gaieties. *It is followed by* The Girl Friend *(1926) and* A Connecticut Yankee *(1927).* |
| 1936–39 | *Three successes in three years showcase Rodgers and Hart's innovations in musical theater:* On Your Toes, Babes in Arms, *and* The Boys from Syracuse. |
| 1943 | *Hart dies. Rodgers writes* Oklahoma! *with Hammerstein and wins his first Pulitzer Prize.* |
| 1948–9 | *Awarded another Pulitzer Prize and nine Tony Awards for* South Pacific. |
| 1959 | *The Sound of Music opens on Broadway.* |
| 1960 | *Hammerstein dies.* |
| 1963–73 | *Collaborates with future stars Stephen Sondheim, Sheldon Harnick, and Martin Charnin.* |
| 1979 | *Dies as* Oklahoma! *returns to a sellout run on Broadway.* |
| 1990 | *Broadway's 46th Street Theater is renamed Richard Rodgers Theater.* |

**FAMOUS TRAINING GROUND**
Rodgers dropped out of Columbia University, New York, to study at the Institute of Musical Art, which later became the renowned Juilliard Music School. Here, as he wrote in his autobiography, he gave up his "losing struggle with Geometry and French" and surrounded himself with "students and teachers whose addiction to music was as great as mine."

**RODGERS AND HART**
All Rodgers' early hits were written with Hart. Many, such as "Blue Moon," "My Funny Valentine," and "Bewitched, Bothered, and Bewildered," are still popular. Hart had a wit that matched the brash, early days of Broadway theater. The partnership was immortalized by Irving Berlin (1888-1989): "Tuneful, tasteful; Soulful, smart; Music: Rodgers; Lyrics: Hart."

Sheet music for *On Your Toes*

**ON YOUR TOES**
Premiered in 1936, this was the first Broadway musical that made dramatic use of classical dance. The climax is the tense jazz ballet *Slaughter on Tenth Avenue*, choreographed by the Russian George Balanchine (1904–83), who later founded the New York City Ballet.

**THE GIRLFRIEND**
Throughout the 1920s, Rodgers and Hart wrote for Broadway and London's West End. This show from 1926 follows a traditional boy-meets-girl pattern. A young farmer and avid cyclist is in love with the daughter of a professional, enters a six-day race, and in the end wins the race and the girl.

"Flapper" brooch, from the 1920s

## RODGERS AND HAMMERSTEIN

n 1943, Richard Rodgers and Oscar Hammerstein egan a hugely successful partnership. Hammerstein ad already distinguished himself as the lyricist for erome Kern's *Show Boat*, as well as in many operettas. ll together, Rodgers and Hammerstein earned 35 Tony wards, 15 Academy Awards, two Pulitzer Prizes, two ƙrammy Awards, and two Emmys.

## SOUTH PACIFIC
A milestone of musical theater, *South Pacific* opened on Broadway in 1948. It was made into a movie starring Mitzi Gaynor and Rossano Brazzi in 1958. It broke new ground by exploring the prejudices between Polynesian islanders and US troops during World War II. This was followed by *The King and I,* in 1951, which explored similar prejudices in the Kingdom of Siam, now Thailand.

Julie Andrews as Maria in the 1965 movie *The Sound of Music*

"*I have a story. I see a stage. I know what my settings are going to be... I sit down and write.*"

**RICHARD RODGERS**
*Coronet* magazine
(US), January 1951

NOW EVERYONE CAN SEE IT AT POPULAR PRICES!

RODGERS & HAMMERSTEIN
PRESENT

**OKLAHOMA!**
CinemaScope
COLOR BY TECHNICOLOR

COMPLETE—INTACT—WITH EVERY SCENE—EVERY SONG OF THE MOTION PICTURE THAT RAN A YEAR ON BROADWAY AT $3.50—!

GORDON MacRAE · GLORIA GRAHAME · SHIRLEY JONES · GENE NELSON
CHARLOTTE GREENWOOD · EDDIE ALBERT · JAMES WHITMORE · ROD STEIGER
RICHARD RODGERS AND OSCAR HAMMERSTEIN II SONYA LEVIEN AND WILLIAM LUDWIG
ARTHUR HORNBLOW, Jr. DIRECTED BY FRED ZINNEMANN AGNES De MILLE
A MAGNA PRODUCTION

## OKLAHOMA!
This was the first of the musicals by Rodgers and Hammerstein, and it pursued more dramatic goals than earlier musicals. The story is about everyday problems faced by everyday people— a young cowboy and a farmer girl and a conflict with her farmhand. It features such memorable songs as: "Oh, What A Beautiful Mornin'" and "People Will Say We're In Love."

Poster for the 1955 film production of *Oklahoma!*

## THE SOUND OF MUSIC
Five of the Rodgers and Hammerstein musicals were made into hit movies, none bigger than *The Sound of Music.* It is based on the story of the von Trapps, a real-life Austrian singing family. Maria comes to be their governess during the early days of the Nazi occupation. Its many songs, such as *Do-Re-Mi* and *Edelweiss*, have become favorites. *Edelweiss* was Hammerstein's last song.

## JOHN COLTRANE
Many of Richard Rodgers' songs have become standards of the pop and jazz world. Famous interpreters of his music include the great jazz saxophonist and composer John Coltrane (1926–67), whose signature tune was *My Favorite Things* from *The Sound of Music.*

# Dmitri Shostakovich

**DMITRI SHOSTAKOVICH (1906–75)**
A painfully shy man who hid behind thick-rimmed glasses, Shostakovich was one of the greatest symphony composers of the 20th century. He was also a prolific film composer with over 30 scores. He relaxed by writing a soccer column for the Russian sports paper, *Red Sport*.

SHOSTAKOVICH WAS AN ENIGMA—someone who shows one face on the outside and says something else on the inside—and that is what makes him endlessly fascinating. He was the greatest composer of Soviet Russia. Shostakovich showed talent very early. When his father died, he helped support his mother and sisters by playing the piano in the movie theater (movies were still silent then). He enrolled at music school, where he excelled at piano and composition. At this time, the Union of Soviet Socialist Republics (USSR) was governed by a cruel dictator, Joseph Stalin (1878–1953). Musicians and writers could only write material approved by the Communist Party. Shostakovich wrote pieces that praised Stalin's regime, and others that secretly mocked its brutality. Many of his symphonies are bold, powerful pieces, full of nationalist fervor, whereas his string quartets are nervous, tentative pieces, written by a man uncertain he could say what he thought.

| | |
|---|---|
| 1906 | September 25, born in St. Petersburg, Russia. His father is a government inspector. |
| 1915 | Takes piano lessons from his mother, an accomplished pianist. |
| 1919 | Admitted to the Leningrad Conservatory, where he studies piano and composition. |
| 1923 | Marries Nina Vasilevna Varzar, mother of his two children. |
| 1926 | First symphony, his graduation piece, premieres to great acclaim. |
| 1930 | Begins opera, Lady Macbeth of the Mtsensk District. It premieres in 1934 in Leningrad and Moscow. |
| 1941 | Composes the first movements of his Symphony No. 7—it becomes a symbol of Nazi resistance. |
| 1953 | Produces his Symphony No. 10 after a long silence of eight years. |
| 1954 | Wife dies. Marries again in 1956, but second marriage does not last. |
| 1959 | Writes first cello concerto and dedicates it to Rostropovich. |
| 1960 | Composes string quartets dedicated To the Memory of the Victims of Fascism and the War. A year later, writes his Symphony No. 12, To the Memory of Lenin. |
| 1962 | Marries Irina Supinskaja. |
| 1966 | Develops a heart condition and is also troubled by severe arthritis. |
| 1975 | Writes Viola Sonata. Dies in Moscow on August 9. |

*Fireman Shostakovich on the cover of* Time *magazine, July 2, 1942*

### SIEGE OF LENINGRAD
In World War II, the German army invaded the USSR and surrounded Leningrad (as St. Petersburg was then called) for 900 days, from 1941 to 1944. During the dark early days of the siege, Shostakovich was a fireman. He also wrote part of his *Symphony No. 7, The Leningrad,* which premiered there in 1942. A copy was smuggled to the West, and Arturo Toscanini conducted a performance in the US that was broadcast to millions.

### THE END OF THE NAZI OCCUPATION
The Soviet army played a key role in defeating the Nazis in World War II. After the war, however, the victorious Soviets became more conservative in their musical tastes. Shostakovich wrote an obligatory "victory" piece, his ninth symphony, which is a merry, mischievous, and amusing work—not what would be expected from a composer coming out of a world war.

## LIFE UNDER STALIN

Shostakovich lived in the USSR under a Communist regime led by Joseph Stalin, one of the most powerful and murderous dictators in history. Stalin was responsible for millions of deaths—especially during the Great Terror of the 1930s, when the leaders purged the country of "enemies of the people." Miraculously, Shostakovich was allowed to continue working, writing symphonies, quartets, operas, and film scores.

*Hammer and sickle are emblems of the Soviet regime*

*Worker and Peasant* sculpture by Vera Mukina, 1937

Rostropovich at the Théatre des Champs-Élysées Paris, 1994

*"Victory of light over darkness, of humanity over barbarism."*

**SHOSTAKOVICH**
describing his *Leningrad Symphony*

## MSTISLAV ROSTROPOVICH

The enormous talent and huge personality of the Russian cellist Rostropovich (1927–2007) won him admirers around the world. Nicknamed "Slava," he studied with Shostakovich, played all his cello works, and was a close friend. A tireless human rights campaigner, he famously wrote to the Russian newspaper *Pravda* defending the dissident writer Alexander Solzhenitsyn. "Since that moment," he said, "my conscience was clean and clear."

## MACBETH WITH A DIFFERENCE

Shostakovich's opera *Lady Macbeth of the Mtsensk District* is a violent opera with plenty of drama. There were over 200 performances before Stalin noisily walked out of one in 1936. The next day's papers condemned it as "chaos instead of music." Shostakovich responded to the criticism by writing his rousing *Symphony No. 5* in 1937, which satisfied the Soviet regime.

Stage version of *Lady Macbeth of Mtsensk*

## TORMENTED COMPOSER

Prokofiev, Shostakovich's contemporary, wrote the classic ballet *Romeo and Juliet* as well as *Peter and the Wolf*, a musical story that introduces children to the instruments of the orchestra (Peter is the strings, and the wolf the French horns). However, like Shostakovich, he fell foul of Stalin's henchmen and was severely criticized. He died on the same day as his tormentor, Stalin.

Sergei Prokofiev (1891–1953)

*Wolves are common subjects in folk tales*

# Leonard Bernstein

**LEONARD BERNSTEIN (1918–90)**
Bernstein's talent and musical curiosity led him to divide his energies between classical music and Broadway shows. He was the first American conductor to build an international career. He led a frenetic social life and was a very vocal supporter of political causes. He really was, as he said, "over-committed on all fronts."

| | |
|---|---|
| 1918 | *August 25, born in Lawrence, Massachusetts. His family were Ukrainian Jewish immigrants.* |
| 1934 | *Enters Harvard University and presents first radio series,* Leonard Bernstein at the Piano. |
| 1940 | *Spends the summer at the major US music venue Tanglewood, as conducting student of Serge Koussevitsky (1874–1951).* |
| 1943 | *Becomes assistant conductor of New York Philharmonic Orchestra (NYP) at the invitation of its music director, Artur Rodzinski. Later becomes the music director.* |
| 1944 | *Premieres* Fancy Free, On the Town, *and* Symphony No. 1. |
| 1953 | *Becomes the first American to conduct at La Scala Opera, Milan, Italy. Premieres* Wonderful Town. |
| 1954 | *Writes score for movie* On the Waterfront *starring Marlon Brando. Writes and performs his first Omnibus broadcast.* |
| 1957 | West Side Story *premieres on Broadway.* |
| 1958 | *First series of* Young People's Concerts, *which continue until 1982 with 53 programs.* |
| 1969 | *Last concert with NYP, making a total of 939 concerts, including 36 world premieres.* |
| 1973 | *His lectures at Harvard are televised in the US and abroad.* |
| 1990 | *Conducts last concert in August. Dies just five days after retiring.* |

THE MOST EXUBERANT AND GIFTED musician of the 20th century, Leonard Bernstein was a major force in every field of music. His versatility in effortlessly embracing both popular and classical music was unique. He contributed dazzling works to American musical theater and created a distinct voice as a composer of works for orchestra and chorus, often combining jazzy rhythms with classical forms. As a conductor, he famously burst on the scene at the age of 25 when he stood in for an ailing elderly conductor, Bruno Walter. The concert with the New York Philharmonic Orchestra was broadcast throughout the US. The next day Bernstein found himself on the front page of the *New York Times*. One of his most enduring legacies was his inspiring series of televised *Young People's Concerts*—for a whole generation, it was an irresistible invitation to great music.

**GOOD THINGS COME IN THREE**
Bernstein had his first hit in 1944 with the all-American ballet *Fancy Free*, at a time when most ballet still came from Europe. This tale of three sailors on leave in New York was made into the musical *On the Town*, which opened on Broadway the same year. The show's success led to a movie version starring Gene Kelly and Frank Sinatra. The film won Bernstein an Academy Award in 1949.

American cowboy, hero of Westerns and ballets

Aaron Copland (1900–90)

**AARON COPLAND**
Bernstein's mentor and musical godfather, Copland paved the way for a generation of American composers. He created a unique musical language that expressed the joys of American folklore. His ballets on American themes—*Appalachian Spring, Rodeo,* and *Billy the Kid*—marked him out as a pioneer. Like Bernstein, he was endlessly enthusiastic in his efforts to bring music to a new generation.

**WEST SIDE STORY**
Based on Shakespeare's *Romeo and Juliet*, this landmark musical tells of two teenage lovers from rival gangs who try to defy racism and violence on the streets of New York to be together. The film version won an astonishing ten Academy Awards. Hit songs like *Tonight, America,* and *Maria* have become classics.

## IN MEMORY OF KENNEDY

Bernstein composed a Mass to celebrate the life of President John F. Kennedy at the request of his widow, Jacqueline. Completed in 1971, it both praised the memory of the president and expressed the anguish that Bernstein and the country felt after his assassination in 1963. The full title is *MASS: A Theater Piece for Singers, Players, and Dancers,* and it combines the performing arts with religious rite.

Kennedy family on cover for *Life* magazine, December 1963

> *"All humans are born with the desire to learn, and to create."*

**BERNSTEIN**
from his book of writings, *The Joy of Music,* published 2004

Conductor's baton

## GIANT OF A CONDUCTOR

Before Bernstein, all the greatest conductors were European. From his early debut in 1943 to his final concerts celebrating the fall of the Berlin Wall, Bernstein's popularity was matched by his unfailing integrity as a great artist. He directed countless orchestras—here, he is shown rehearsing the London Symphony Orchestra. In addition to his historic leadership of the New York Philharmonic, Bernstein had a very close relationship with the Israel Philharmonic Orchestra.

Scene from 1961 movie *West Side Story,* choreographed by Jerome Robbins

# Ali Akbar Khan

**ALI AKBAR KHAN (b. 1922)**
Khan has worked tirelessly for many years to bring Indian musical traditions to a wider audience. He has achieved this not only through performances around the world as a virtuoso *sarod* player, but also through the schools of Indian music he founded in India, Switzerland, and California.

| | |
|---|---|
| 1922 | *April 14, born in village of Shibpur, East Bengal (Bangladesh).* |
| 1925 | *Begins music studies, singing with father and drumming with uncle.* |
| 1935 | *Gives first public performances.* |
| 1944 | *Makes his first recording for the HMV record label.* |
| 1945 | *Becomes court musician to the Maharaja of Jodhpur.* |
| 1955 | *Visits the US at the request of Yehudi Menuhin (1916–99). Makes the first recording of Indian music in the West, and appears on Alistair Cooke's* Omnibus. |
| 1956 | *Founds Ali Akbar College of Music in Calcutta, India.* |
| 1960 | *Composes film score for Satyajit Ray's* Devi. |
| 1967 | *Founds Ali Akbar College of Music in Marin County, California.* |
| 1970 | *Nominated for Grammy for* Shree Rag. |
| 1971 | *Receives Monterey Jazz Festival gold disc for* Concert for Bangladesh. |
| 1988 | *Receives Padma Bhusan award—the highest civilian honor in India.* |
| 1991 | *Becomes the first Indian musician to receive MacArthur Foundation Fellowship ("genius grant").* |
| 1994 | *Composes film score for Bernardo Bertolucci's* Little Buddha. |

**I**NDIA HAS A DISTINGUISHED TRADITION of classical music based on holy texts, and one of its greatest virtuosos is Ali Akbar Khan. Like many other great musicians around the world, Khan comes from a musical family. He trained as a singer from the age of three, but his instrument is the *sarod*. This is rather like a big guitar with an additional dozen or so strings that just resonate, creating the characteristic "halo" of sound. Traditionally, Indian music was never written down. Instead, it was passed down aurally from generation to generation.

As a boy, Khan practiced for up to 18 hours a day memorizing music. He also studied Western music notation, and was a pioneer in the preservation of Indian music in written form, which he continues through his music schools around the world.

Palace at Jodhpur

**COURT MUSICIAN AT JODHPUR**
Ali Akbar Khan can trace his family back to a musician at the 16th-century court of Emperor Akbar. Khan himself was court musician to the Maharaja of Jodhpur for seven years. The state of Jodhpur bestowed on him the honor of *Ustad*, or Master Musician. He has also been honored by the United Nations and the US government.

*"For us, as a family, music is like food. When you need it you don't have to explain why, because it is basic to life."*

**KHAN**
describing his music tradition on his website

Sanskrit text from late 19th century on a roll of silk

**HINDU SCRIPTURE**
The classical music of North India dates back to the 12th century. It was based on sacred Hindu texts written in sanskrit, called *Vedas*. The music, which originated from the north of the Indian subcontinent, was influenced by Persian (Iranian) music. The player or singer interprets a sequence of notes called the *raga*, and the performance is usually marked by long improvisations.

Richly decorated bowl, or soundbox, made from a gourd

## TRADITIONAL INDIAN INSTRUMENTS

Indian music is based on vocal performance, but instrumental music has existed since antiquity. Indian instruments are plucked, blown, and struck, roughly like western string, wind, and percussion instruments. The popular *sitar*, *sarod*, and *sarangi* have principal strings that are plucked or bowed, and "sympathetic" strings that resonate (vibrate through the instrument) to give a shimmering sound.

*Sitar*, or Indian lute

*Arched frets for principal strings*

*Turning pegs for the sympathetic strings under frets*

*Player presses strings against frets like a guitarist*

*Pegs secure the main strings*

Bollywood movie poster for *Umrao Jaan* (1981), which featured the songs of Asha Bhosle

## BOLLYWOOD MOVIE MUSIC

India produces more movies than any other country. The Indian film industry is nicknamed "Bollywood," after Hollywood and Bombay. The majority of Bollywood movies are musicals, and most professional composers and musicians have had some contact with the industry. Many Indian singers, such as Asha Bhosle, have recorded songs for movies. Ali Akbar Khan has written film music both in India and in the West.

*Sympathetic strings thread through holes in fingerboard*

Indian *sarangi*

*Player passes a bow over the strings*

Zakir Hussain (b. 1951)

Tabla *player hits center of the skin*

*Waisted body made from one block of wood*

## JOHN McLAUGHLIN

The improvisation in Indian music appeals strongly to jazz musicians, as do its spiritual qualities. The US jazz guitarist John McLaughlin (b. 1927) began his career with Miles Davis. He has experimented with Indian music in his Mahavishnu Orchestra, and with his group Shakti. McLaughlin's groups have included outstanding Indian musicians like Zakir Hussain and L. Shankar.

## INDIAN MUSICAL COLLABORATION

Khan has worked with the most talented Indian musicians. Percussionist Zakir Hussain, one of the greatest *tabla* (Indian percussion instrument) players, has often performed with Khan. So has the *sitar* player and composer Ravi Shankar (b. 1920) and the violinist L. Subramaniam (b. 1947), who has composed pieces that combine symphony orchestras with Indian traditions.

# Pierre Boulez

NOBODY HAS MADE such an impression in the world of contemporary concert music as Pierre Boulez. For 40 years he has been active as a composer, conductor, broadcaster, and teacher. Gifted at math and engineering, he chose instead to study music in Paris. Boulez was eager to explore the latest innovations in music and was often disappointed that contemporary musicians did not share his zeal for innovation. This led, in 1954, to him starting a series of new-music concerts called *Le Domaine Musical* at the Théâtre Marigny, Paris, where he was music director. The concerts ran for over a decade. They revolutionized Parisian musical life, and gave Boulez a unique opportunity to try out new ideas as conductor, composer, and concert promoter.

**PIERRE BOULEZ (b. 1925)**
Boulez is a musical explorer and adventurer who goes where no other composers have gone before. His early pieces carried forward the innovations of Arnold Schoenberg. As an outstanding conductor, he has premiered new works by countless living composers.

| | |
|---|---|
| 1925 | *March 26, born in Montbrison, France.* |
| 1944 | *Studies math at Lyon University, then changes to study with Olivier Messiaen at Paris Conservatoire.* |
| 1952 | *Publishes* Schoenberg is Dead, *which attacks complacency in new music.* |
| 1954 | *Founds* Le Domaine Musical *series of concerts.* |
| 1955 | *Premieres his most famous piece,* Le marteau sans maître *(The Masterless Hammer).* |
| 1960 | *Premieres* Pli selon pli *(Fold by Fold), for soprano and orchestra.* |
| 1963 | *Conducts first performance in France of Austrian composer Alban Berg's opera,* Wozzeck. |
| 1969 | *Becomes principal guest conductor of the Chicago Symphony Orchestra.* |
| 1971 | *Succeeds Bernstein at the New York Philharmonic Orchestra and becomes chief conductor of the BBC Symphony Orchestra.* |
| 1976 | *Founds the IRCAM Ensemble Intercontemporain. Conducts* Wagner's Ring Cycle *at Bayreuth.* |
| 1977 | *Opens the IRCAM at the Pompidou Centre, Paris.* |
| 1982 | *Premiere of* Répons *which uses IRCAM technology at BBC Proms in London and is awarded a Grammy for it in 2000.* |
| 2003 | *Publishes* Boulez on Conducting. |

**TAUGHT BY A MASTER**
Olivier Messiaen (1908–92) taught Boulez at the Paris Conservatoire. He was a unique figure in music, as he was a superb composer and a great ornithologist (expert on birds). As a composer, he notated the songs of hundreds of birds and used them in his vivid, exotic music.

*"Music is a labyrinth with no beginning and no end, full of new paths to discover, where mystery remains eternal."*

**BOULEZ**
describing his feelings about music

*Player slides a ring along the keyboard*

*Bottom is traditional speaker, top contains strings that give a halo of sound*

*Ondes martenot played by Ginette Martenot*

**ONDES MARTENOT**
This is one of the earliest electronic instruments. It was invented by Maurice Martenot in 1928, and is played here by his sister, Ginette. The haunting sound of the *ondes martenot* was used to greatest effect by Messiaen in works such as his *Turangalila-Symphonie.* It is also popular with film composers—it featured in *Lawrence of Arabia* (1962) and *Ghostbusters* (1984).

## UNIQUE RESEARCH CENTER
Boulez has always been fascinated with the potential of electronic instruments. In 1970, the French president, Georges Pompidou, asked him to set up an institution for this research. The result was IRCAM (*Institut de Recherche et Coordination Acoustique/Musique*—Institute for the Research and Performance of Electroacoustic Music). IRCAM also has its own world-famous ensemble.

Wagner's *Ring Cycle* at Bayreuth, 1976

*Wall covered with superabsorbent acoustic padding soundproofs the room*

Recording room at IRCAM

## CONDUCTOR OF WAGNER OPERAS
Boulez's creativity as a conductor has had an enormous influence on the kind of music we hear and the quality of its performance. Few other conductors have done more to clarify orchestral playing. Although Boulez is well known for his modern music, his work with French director Patrice Chéreau on this production of Wagner's *Ring Cycle* at Bayreuth, and their recordings of it, are famous.

## MUSICAL SPACE
One of Boulez's boldest pieces, called *Répons* (*Responses*), aims to recreate in sound the relationships that we experience with the space around us. When *Répons* is performed, the audience sits between the orchestra and the soloists. Boulez compares the sensation to walking through the Guggenheim, whose interior features a spiral ramp that runs from top to bottom. Here a person can see behind, in front, and across the building at the same time.

*Under a glass dome, visitors walk along a continuous "ramp" to view works of art*

The Guggenheim Museum, New York

## PASSION FOR PERCUSSION
The use of percussion as an important solo instrument is a relatively recent development. Most 20th-century composers, including Boulez, have given percussion a prominent role in a performance. It is often used to punctuate the rhythms of a piece and, through the use of ethnic instruments from around the world, it can give an exotic flavor to music.

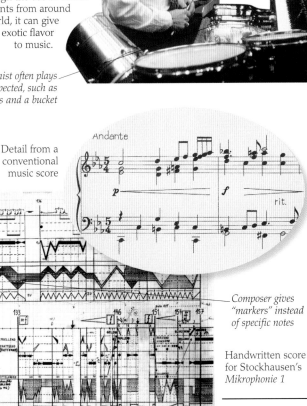

*Percussionist often plays the unexpected, such as bottles and a bucket*

Detail from a conventional music score

## STOCKHAUSEN
Boulez was one of a group of composers who championed new ways of writing music. Some of them tried to write down their musical intentions with drawings instead of notes. This gave performers the freedom to choose what they play. One of the group was German composer Karlheinz Stockhausen (b. 1928). Shown here is his percussion piece for an amplified tam-tam (large gong).

*Composer gives "markers" instead of specific notes*

Handwritten score for Stockhausen's *Mikrophonie 1*

# Toru Takemitsu

A TINY, DELICATE MAN, who stood just over 5 ft (1.5 m) high, Takemitsu was a giant in international contemporary music. Largely self-taught, he wrote hundreds of works for the concert platform, as well as 93 film scores and a detective novel. He also loved popular culture and had an encyclopedic knowledge of Western pop music. As a young man, Takemitsu had a long illness, and lay for several years in bed listening to postwar American military radio. This instilled a knowledge and love of jazz and of Western classical music, so much so that he initially shunned traditional Japanese music. Only gradually did Takemitsu begin to acknowledge traditional Japanese culture in his music.

| | |
|---|---|
| 1930 | *October 8, born in Tokyo, Japan, then moves to China, with his family.* |
| 1944 | *Completes Japanese military service, which left him bitter, but gave him contact with Western music.* |
| 1951 | *Founds an experimental workshop, Jikken Kobo, that avoids Japanese art.* |
| 1955 | *Begins to use electronic tape-recording techniques.* |
| 1957 | Requiem for Strings *wins acclaim from Stravinsky.* |
| 1961 | *First hears music by John Cage.* |
| 1966 | *Receives commission from abroad—* Dorian Horizon. *It is performed by the San Francisco Symphony, conducted by Aaron Copland.* |
| 1967 | *Composes* November Steps *for New York Philharmonic Orchestra. Integrates Japanese instruments into the orchestra.* |
| 1970 | *Meets many western composers at Expo '70 in Japan. Commissioned to write for* Gagaku *ensemble.* |
| 1972 | *Visits Bali. Its gamelan music has a lasting influence on him.* |
| 1977 | *Writes best-known piece,* A Flock Descends into the Pentagonal Garden. *Arranges classic pop songs for guitar:* 12 Songs for Guitar. |
| 1994 | *Wins US Grawemeyer Award for music composition.* |
| 1996 | *Dies of pneumonia.* |

## EAST MEETS WEST
Takemitsu's early musical tastes ranged from Olivier Messiaen and Duke Ellington to a strong affinity for the French composer Claude Debussy (1862–1918). "I am self-taught, but I consider Debussy my teacher," Takemitsu declared. Debussy was very attracted to the restrained and delicate beauty of this picture by the Japanese artist Hokusai, which he used on the front cover of his masterpiece *La Mer* (*The Sea*).

Original cover for Debussy's *La Mer* (*The Sea*), 1905

> "I have recognized my own culture through studying modern Western music."

**TAKEMITSU**
describing the inspiration for his work

Cage with his "prepared" piano

## JOHN CAGE
It was the avant-garde American composer John Cage (1912–92) who first suggested that Takemitsu look again at his Japanese heritage. Takemitsu was influenced by Cage's use of "chance" procedures, in which some details of a piece were left up to the performer. Cage's exotic music for "prepared" piano made a big impression on Takemitsu. A "prepared" piano has screws, rubber bands, and chains on its strings, which turns it into a percussion instrument.

Notched
mouthpiece

*Shakuhachi,* or Japanese
notch flute

*Hollowed bamboo*

## JAPANESE INSTRUMENTS

Gradually Takemitsu wove traditional sounds into his music. *November Steps* is a concerto for *biwa* (Japanese lute), *shakuhachi* (bamboo flute), and orchestra. *Autumn Garden* was written for *Gagaku*, the traditional Japanese orchestra. It has a haunting melody using *ryteiki* (flutes), *hichiriki*, and *sho* (reed instruments), backed by mouth organs and drums.

*Biwa*
player

## LOVE OF NATURE

Takemitsu loved to compare composing and listening to music with walking through Japanese gardens. He painted this picture most vividly when describing his piece for piano and orchestra, *Arc:* "The orchestra represents the sand, rocks, trees, and grass. The piano assumes the role of the wanderer."

## SEIJI OZAWA

Ozawa (b. 1935) is the first postwar Japanese conductor to build an international career. Initially a pianist, he switched to conducting after a rugby injury. He came to Europe, where he met Leonard Bernstein. Ozawa eventually become music director of the Boston Symphony Orchestra in the US. Ozawa and Takemitsu were close friends, recording *November Steps* together.

*Samurai
warriors*

## MOVIE MUSIC

Takemitsu wrote the music for such Japanese classics as Kurosawa's *Ran* (1985), which was based on Shakespeare's epic story *King Lear*. His film music was as important to him as his concert music. He boasted that he saw around 300 films a year, including Hollywood blockbusters, Westerns, art movies, and trash. He said: "I learn a great deal about people… By watching them in the movies, I can get a sense of their feelings and their inner lives."

Battle scene from *Ran*, the most expensive Japanese movie ever made

**PHILIP GLASS (b. 1937)**

Glass was one of the early minimalist composers whose music was marked by a steady, unchanging pulse, repetitive melodies, and harmonies that changed slowly over a long period. He has now shaken off this tag and writes technically demanding music of increasing drama and depth.

| | |
|---|---|
| 1937 | *January 31, born in Baltimore, Maryland.* |
| 1952 | *Attends University of Chicago to study mathematics and philosophy, but switches to music.* |
| 1957 | *Enrolls at the Juilliard Music School in New York, and in 1959 is awarded a student composer prize.* |
| 1963 | *Studies in Paris with Nadia Boulanger and sees new plays at Barrault's Odéon Theatre and films by French New Wave directors.* |
| 1967 | *Forms his Philip Glass Ensemble in New York, and takes lessons in Indian music.* |
| 1970 | *Composes many pieces for the theater group Mabou Mines.* |
| 1976 | *Opera* Einstein on the Beach *premieres in Europe and at the Metropolitan Opera, New York.* |
| 1980 | *Premieres opera* Satyagraha. |
| 1982 | *Writes music for the film* Koyaanisqatsi: Life Out of Balance—*the first of 80 film scores.* |
| 1987 | *Writes a violin concerto, which signals a new use of traditional forms, and goes on to compose symphonies and string quartets.* |
| 2001 | *Carnegie Hall and Brucknerhaus Linz co-commission* Symphony No. 6 *for his 60th birthday.* |
| 2005 | *Premieres his opera* Waiting for the Barbarians *and* Symphony No. 8. |

# Philip Glass

ONE OF THE BEST KNOWN and most prolific modern composers, Philip Glass was introduced to music through his father's radio repair shop. The shop also sold records, and Glass's father often took discs home to play to his three children. These included recordings of the great chamber works, so the future composer rapidly became familiar with Beethoven quartets and Schubert sonatas, as well as Shostakovich symphonies. Glass became serious about music in his teens and went to study it at the University of Chicago, supporting himself with part-time jobs waiting tables and loading airplanes. He rebelled against the fashion among his contemporaries for atonal music, which had limited popular appeal, and began to write music that captivated a large new audience.

**TIBETAN BUDDHISM**

Glass has forged a particularly close relationship with the music of India and Tibet. Glass became a Buddhist and is committed to supporting the Tibetan people. He helps organize the annual Tibet House Freedom Gig in New York, as China does not allow the festival to be held on Tibetan soil.

**NADIA BOULANGER**

After leaving New York, Glass studied with the famous French teacher Nadia Boulanger (1887–1979), whose many other students included Aaron Copland and Quincy Jones. Glass benefited from her rigid discipline, but he disliked the emphasis on atonal music, which only drew small audiences. It did, however, help him discover the type of music he wanted to write.

**OPERAS GALORE**

When Glass sets words to music, they are heard very clearly, making his work particularly suitable for opera. He has composed over 20 operas, including an early group of three works portraying men who changed our world: *Einstein on the Beach* features scientist Albert Einstein; *Satyagraha* portrays Mahatma Gandhi, the father of nonviolent protest; and *Akhnaten* is based on the life of the ancient Egyptian pharaoh.

Tulku Jamyang Kunga Tenzin as the five-year-old Dalai Lama in *Kundun* (1997)

**FILM MUSIC**

Glass's greatest exposure has been as a composer for films. His early scores included the trilogy *Koyaanisqatsi, Powaqqatsi,* and *Naqoyqatsi,* which examined humanity's relationship with the environment. The films used dramatic time-lapse photography to striking effect with Glass's repetitive music. He has worked with directors such as Martin Scorsese on *Kundun* and Stephen Daldry on *The Hours* (2002).

*"What came to me as a revelation was the use of rhythm in developing an overall structure in music."*

**GLASS** on his website, talking about what inspires him

*Wooden tuning pegs*

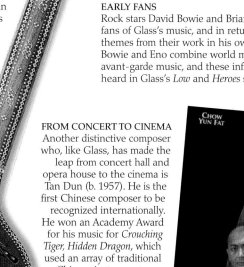
David Bowie

Indian *tambura*, a type of lute

*Egyptian Hamza El Din playing with the Kronos at a peace concert*

### PATH TO INDIAN MUSIC
While studying in Paris, Glass was asked to work with sitarist Ravi Shankar, transcribing his music into western notation so that local classical musicians could play it. This was the key that helped Glass to find his own musical language. He took lessons in Indian music, which features much repetition, with new rhythms and harmonies gradually added over time.

### EARLY FANS
Rock stars David Bowie and Brian Eno were fans of Glass's music, and in return Glass used themes from their work in his own symphonies. Bowie and Eno combine world music, rock, and avant-garde music, and these influences can be heard in Glass's *Low* and *Heroes* symphonies.

### KRONOS STRING QUARTET
Central to Glass's output is a group of five string quartets that have been recorded by the Kronos String Quartet. This group is unique in playing all types of music for string quartet—jazz, avant-garde, folk music, even Jimi Hendrix's *Purple Haze.* They have also performed Glass's new score for the 1931 film *Dracula.*

*Player plucks the strings*

*Ivory bridge supports strings*

CHOW YUN FAT   MICHELLE YEOH   CHANG CHEN

### FROM CONCERT TO CINEMA
Another distinctive composer who, like Glass, has made the leap from concert hall and opera house to the cinema is Tan Dun (b. 1957). He is the first Chinese composer to be recognized internationally. He won an Academy Award for his music for *Crouching Tiger, Hidden Dragon,* which used an array of traditional Chinese instruments, as well as the full arsenal of orchestral instruments.

*Alan Oke as Mahatma Gandhi in* Satyagraha *at London's Coliseum, 2007*

*Paintings depict Hindu god Rama and his wife Sita*

Movie poster for *Crouching Tiger, Hidden Dragon* (2000)

TIGRE & DRAGON
UN FILM DE ANG LEE
SELECTION OFFICIELLE CANNES 2000

# The Beatles

JOHN, PAUL, GEORGE, AND RINGO together made up the group that epitomized the 1960s—the decade when pop music changed the world. The Beatles led the way with their music, clothes, and style. They started in Liverpool, UK, as a skiffle group (folk band influenced by jazz and blues), but their main inspiration came from US pop stars like Elvis Presley. There are many stories about the origin of the group's name; the most popular is that they started as The Silver Beetles, shortened the name, and changed the spelling to "Beatles" in 1960. John and Paul wrote their early hits "Love Me Do" and "Please Please Me." Soon afterward, a tidal wave of popularity swept across the ocean to America with the US release of "She Loves You" and "I Want to Hold Your Hand."

### THE BEATLES
John, George, and Paul first played together in 1958 as the Quarrymen, named after the Quarry Bank Grammar School attended by John Lennon. Ringo joined in 1962, when they were offered an engagement in Hamburg, Germany. They were nicknamed "the moptops" because of their hairstyle.

| | |
|---|---|
| 1940 | July 7, Ringo Starr (Richard Starkey) and October 9, John Lennon born in Liverpool, England. |
| 1942 | June 18, Paul McCartney born in Liverpool. George Harrison born Feb. 25, 1943. |
| 1956 | John Lennon's mother buys him a guitar and he forms the first Quarrymen. |
| 1957 | Lennon meets McCartney and asks him to join the group. Harrison joins a year later. |
| 1961 | Performance at the Cavern Club in Liverpool. Record store manager Brian Epstein takes them on. |
| 1962 | Ringo joins the group as drummer, and they have first recording session at London's EMI Studios. |
| 1964 | Have their first US hit, "I Want To Hold Your Hand." Appear on US television's Ed Sullivan Show. |
| 1965 | The Queen awards them with Britain's prestigious MBE. |
| 1966 | Announce final tour at San Francisco's Candlestick Park. |
| 1967 | Release album Sgt. Pepper's Lonely Hearts Club Band. |
| 1968 | Interest in Indian music and culture develops. Found company Apple Corps, Ltd. in London. |
| 1969 | Last performance together during the filming of Let It Be. |
| 1970 | Paul McCartney announces he is leaving; group is dissolved in 1975. |

George Martin, seated
(b. 1926)

### THE FIFTH BEATLE
A producer is the person who helps a band focus on their musical strengths. The Beatles' producer, George Martin, was often called "the fifth Beatle." He spotted the band's raw talent and offered to produce them after they were turned down by Decca Records. Their business manager, Brian Epstein (1934–67), had been told by a record company: "Guitar bands are on the way out, Mr. Epstein."

*"It was like being in the eye of a hurricane. You'd wake up in a concert and think, 'Wow, how did I get here?'"*

**JOHN LENNON**
after The Beatles' first concerts in New York, 1963

### BEATLEMANIA
Nobody had ever seen anything like the hysteria for The Beatles in the 1960s. Thousands of adoring, screaming fans (mostly girls) followed them everywhere they went—police and ambulances were always on hand. In 1964, The Beatles were the first "supergroup" to perform a sellout concert packed with nearly 60,000 at New York's Shea Stadium.

### TELSTAR SATELLIT
The 1960s was an era of change, an pop songs reflect this. The Telsta communications satellite wa launched in 1962, and marked b a hit single of the same name by British band called The Tornados They were the first British band t get to number one in the US charts The Beatles followed soon afte

McCartney and Lennon on the set of *The Ed Sullivan Show,* February 1964

## RECORD-BREAKING SONGWRITERS
Beatles songwriters Lennon and McCartney created an outstanding catalog of music. In 1964, The Beatles held the top five US chart places—a position never since bettered. McCartney has had 32 number one hits in the US and Lennon 26. There are 3,000 recorded versions of *Yesterday,* making it the most "covered" (recorded by other people) song in history.

*McCartney's left-handed bass guitar*

*Lennon's distinctive* Rickenbacker *guitar*

Ravi Shankar playing his *sitar*

## ABBEY ROAD
The Beatles recorded almost all their singles and albums between 1962 and 1970 at their recording company EMI's Abbey Road studios in London. The cover of their famous album *Abbey Road* publicized the studio, which has become a pilgrimage point for Beatles fans. Their first live satellite broadcast from Abbey Road in 1967, performing "All You Need Is Love," was seen by an estimated 400 million worldwide.

## EASTERN FASCINATION
Beatles guitarist George Harrison was the first to use Indian classical music in pop records after he became a fan of *sitar* master Ravi Shankar (b. 1920). The Beatles embraced the fashionable search for spiritual enlightenment from the East. Their *guru* (religious teacher) was the Maharishi Mahesh Yogi, whose followers included many pop stars and celebrities.

Toy Beatles in their yellow submarine

## BEATLES ON FILM
As well as records, The Beatles produced many films that featured their music, including the zany *A Hard Day's Night* (1964) and *Help!* (1965). At the height of the psychedelic phase of the 1960s they released their first animated film, *Yellow Submarine* (1968). It was a box-office hit, with its wild, adventurous images and soundtrack of wacky songs.

# Bob Dylan

**BOB DYLAN (b. 1941)**
The ancient Greeks sang their poems. Medieval troubadours traveled from town to town spreading the news with songs. Bob Dylan did much the same, but his poems, or songs, told about people, events, and issues that struck a chord with a generation growing up in the 1960s. He has written around 450 songs since 1962.

| | |
|---|---|
| 1941 | *May 24, born Robert Zimmerman, in Duluth, Minnesota.* |
| 1959 | *Starts performing in a local coffee house, singing folk and blues.* |
| 1961 | *After reading Woody Guthrie's* Bound for Glory, *Dylan moves to New York City to meet him.* |
| 1962 | *Writes "Blowin' in the Wind," the anthem of the civil rights movement.* |
| 1963 | *Releases album* Freewheelin' Bob Dylan *and performs at New York and Newport folk festivals.* |
| 1965 | *Starts using electric guitar at the Newport Folk Festival.* |
| 1966 | *Crashes his Triumph motorcycle and stops touring for several years.* |
| 1967 | *Releases country-tinged album* John Wesley Harding, *featuring "All Along the Watchtower."* |
| 1969 | Nashville Skyline *completes transformation to country singer.* |
| 1974 | *Comeback tour with The Band is hailed as a success.* |
| 1976 | *Martin Scorsese makes* The Last Waltz, *about farewell concert of The Band, Dylan's backing group.* |
| 1980 | *Wins first Grammy Awards for* Gotta Serve Somebody. |
| 1985 | *In between tours, helps out at Live Aid concert in Philadelphia.* |
| 1988 | *Begins "Never Ending Tour."* |
| 2007 | *Biographical film* I'm Not There *is released.* |

**T**HIS MAN FROM THE AMERICAN MIDWEST quite simply changed the face of popular music. He fused American folk, blues, country music, and rock 'n' roll. Dylan was attracted to folk music early on, especially the music of folk hero Woody Guthrie (1912–67), writer of "This Land Is Your Land" and the archetypal traveling musician. In New York's Greenwich Village, Dylan created a modern kind of folk music, one that put folk, country, and blues to the underground poetry of 1950s and 1960s. He wrote songs about the Cold War, the war in Vietnam, and the growing divisions within American society.

**MARTIN LUTHER KING JR. (1929–68)**
In 1963, more than 200,000 demonstrators gathered in Washington, DC, to protest for jobs and freedom for African Americans. The climax was the "I have a dream..." speech by civil rights activist Martin Luther King Jr.—now one of the landmark speeches of the 20th century. Dylan and Joan Baez both performed on the day.

**LONG COLLABORATION**
Early in his career, Dylan forged a partnership with folk singer Joan Baez (b. 1941). He said, "There was no one like her... However illogical it seemed, something told me that she was my counterpart." The two performed together, worked on films, and took part in many US civil rights marches.

Poster for 1978 film *Renaldo and Clara* by Bob Dylan, co-starring his wife Sara and Joan Baez

*"The folk music scene had been like a paradise that I had to leave, like Adam had to leave the garden. It was just too perfect."*

**DYLAN**
in the first volume of his autobiography, *Chronicles*, published 2004

**CONCERT PERFORMER**
Dylan has been touring since the 1960s, although he stopped for several years after a motorcycle accident. Always enigmatic and intense, he has changed styles repeatedly, veering from folk to electric rock, from born-again Christian to Country and Western, always a step ahead of his fans. He still plays about 100 concerts a year.

**MICHAEL JACKSON (b. 1958)**
Known as "the King of Pop," Michael Jackson became an instant star at age 11 as the youngest member of the family group, the Jackson Five. His solo career dominated the pop charts and airwaves around the world throughout the 1980s and 90s, before ending in controversy.

# Michael Jackson

**JACKSON HAS WORKED WITH EVERYONE** from Diana Ross to Homer Simpson. He has enthralled his worldwide audience with dancing skills that put him in a tradition of great entertainers like Fred Astaire. Jackson is a singer, songwriter, record producer, arranger, actor, and choreographer. He is one of the best-selling artists of all time and has given millions of dollars to charity. Jackson's career is a catalog of achievement: he has received 13 Grammy Awards and has had 13 number-one chart singles in the US. He has been named the "Most Successful Entertainer of All Time" by Guinness World Records.

**JACKSON FIVE**
Michael is one of 10 children, all of whom showed a musical talent that was fostered by their father. Touring in a group with his older brothers taught Michael performance skills, musicianship, and the value of sheer hard work. In 1976, he became their songwriter with hits like "Shake Your Body" and "Can You Feel It."

| | |
|---|---|
| 1958 | *August 29, born in Gary, Indiana.* |
| 1964 | *Joins group formed by his brothers, which becomes The Jackson Five.* |
| 1971 | *Releases first solo single, "Got to Be There."* |
| 1972 | *"Ben," the title song from a film about a rat, becomes his first solo number one chart single.* |
| 1979 | *Just after 21st birthday, releases* Off the Wall. *It is in the Top Ten for eight months and produces four hit singles.* |
| 1982 | *Narrates a storybook album for* E. T.: The Extraterrestrial. Thriller *is released in December and tops the album charts for 37 weeks in 1983. The Making of Michael Jackson's Thriller is the best-selling music home video.* |
| 1984 | *Wins eight Grammys, eight American music awards, and three MTV awards.* |
| 1987 | *Releases "I Just Can't Stop Loving You" with Siedah Garret and "Bad," which tops charts for eight weeks.* |
| 1991 | *Controversial "Black or White" video debuts on television—a teaser for next album,* Dangerous. |
| 1993 | *Gives halftime performance at Superbowl XXVII.* |
| 2000 | Thriller *receives its 26th platinum award, having sold 26 million copies in the US alone.* |
| 2001 | *Is inducted into the Rock and Roll Hall of Fame. Releases* Invincible. |

**BEST-SELLING ALBUMS**
After Jackson's huge success with *Off the Wall,* he and producer Quincy Jones teamed up for what would become the best-selling record of all time—*Thriller.* To date, the album has sold 51 million copies. It has produced an amazing seven hit singles, and it remained in the US top 100 for over two years. The *Thriller* music video is the also the most famous (and, at 14 minutes, the longest) ever produced.

*"Michael's a natural. He's a very hard worker and a super performer. But most of all, he's a real human being."*

**STEVIE WONDER (b. 1950)**

*Jackson performing his "Moonwalk" in New York in 1997*

**MOONWALK**
Jackson gave an electrifying performance of the hit "Billie Jean" on the Motown 25th-anniversary TV special in May 1983. He launched his gravity-defying trademark "Moonwalk" before a global audience of 50 million. Quincy Jones told *Time* magazine, "Black music had to play second fiddle for a long time, but its spirit is the whole motor of pop. Michael has connected with every soul in the world."

# Gilberto Passos Gil Moreira

**GILBERTO PASSOS GIL MOREIRA (b. 1942)**
Brazil's superstar Gilberto Gil has performed around the world and is responsible for laying the foundation for the modern Brazilian music *Tropicalia*. Alongside a political career, he has released 65 albums, sold over four million records, and has 12 gold records and five platinum albums.

MANY POP STARS dabble in politics, but only a few devote themselves to the job of changing government. Gilberto Gil is now the Brazilian Minister for Culture. He grew up in the 1960s playing bossa nova (a mix of traditional Brazilian samba, and jazz) and listening to The Beatles. In 1968, his song lyrics criticizing the Brazilian military government of the day landed him in prison. He was subsequently exiled from Brazil, so he set off for London in pursuit of a solo career. Gil is one of Brazil's greatest musicians and a champion of World Music—modern folk music that combines traditional styles of music from around the world.

**POLITICAL PROTEST**
Gil's great friend and collaborator is Caetano Veloso (b. 1942), who with Gil helped create the music style *Tropicalia*. Like Gil, Caetano took part in anti-government protests in the 1960s. He too was imprisoned and exiled. Caetano has since become an internationally recognized solo performer.

*"I've gone from being the stone thrower to the glass...That's the way life is: you move from one state of things to another."*

**GIL**
London's *Observer* newspaper, October 19, 2003

| | |
|---|---|
| **1942** | June 26, born in San Salvador, Bahia, Brazil. In teens begins music career as a bossa nova musician. |
| **1967** | Is inspired by The Beatles and other English-language rock musicians. Music movement Tropicalia is born—a fusion of bossa nova, rock, local folk music, African traditions, and Portuguese sea shanties. |
| **1968** | Brazilian military government grants dictatorial powers to the president. Gil joins anti-government protests and is jailed. |
| **1969** | Is released from prison and exiled. Travels to London, England. |
| **1970s** | Tours US and performs with reggae artist Jimmy Cliff. Returns to Brazil and helps introduce reggae to his homeland. |
| **1980** | Releases version of reggae artist Bob Marley's No Woman, No Cry. |
| **1998** | Wins Grammy award for Quanta Live. |
| **2002** | Caetano Veloso publishes book about the new music movement: Tropical Truth: A Story of Music and Revolution in Brazil. |
| **2003** | Becomes Brazil's Minister of Culture under President da Silva. |
| **2005** | Wins seventh Grammy for Electracústico. Is also awarded Sweden's Polar Music Prize and the French Légion d'Honneur. |

Pink Floyd

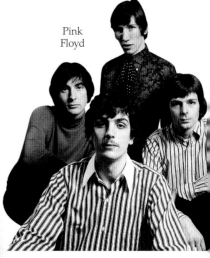

**MUSICAL INFLUENCES**
When Gil was exiled from Brazil, he headed for the epicenter of pop music—London. He played with groups such as Yes, Pink Floyd, and the Incredible String Band, while continuing his solo career. On his return to Brazil he combined European pop and Caribbean reggae to create passionate music that matched his strong social convictions.

*Traditional Brazilian samba dancer*

**BRAZILIAN CARNIVAL**
Rio de Janeiro, capital of Brazil, is home to the world famous annual Carnival that takes place 40 days before Easter. Hundreds of spectacular floats surrounded by dancers, singers, and drummers dressed in elaborate costumes parade through the streets. Gil is an avid promoter of Carnival as the people's way of expressing their joy through music.

# Youssou N'Dour

A MUSICIAN, ACTOR, AND UNICEF AMBASSADOR, Youssou N'Dour is the most recognized voice of Africa. His dynamic music combines the traditional African *griot* singing (a kind of religious praising, accompanied by traditional percussion), with Afro-Cuban styles from Latin America and rock music from the US. This infectious sound, known as *mbalax,* has carried N'Dour's voice around the world. He started performing as a boy on the streets of his native Dakar. His first African success was with his group Etoile de Dakar (Star of Dakar). Since then, N'Dour has led campaigns to combat the spread of malaria in Africa and increase access to technology. He set up an eco-movement called *Set-Seetal* (Be Clean) to improve housing and sanitation in his native Senegal.

| | |
|---|---|
| 1959 | October 1, born in Dakar, Senegal into a family of griot singers. |
| 1971 | Begins performing in groups on the streets of Dakar. |
| 1979 | Forms his own ensemble, Etoile de Dakar (Star of Dakar), and achieves first success performing with a Latin-African beat. |
| 1984 | Founds group Super Etoile de Dakar (Dakar Superstar), whose success spreads his music across Africa and into Europe. |
| 1988 | Features on the Amnesty International Human Rights Now! tour with Lou Reed. |
| 1991 | Is appointed a goodwill ambassador for Unicef (United Nations Children's Fund). |
| 1994 | Takes part in Africa Opéra at the Palais Garnier, Paris. |
| 1994 | Has a global hit with song "Seven Seconds" with singer Neneh Cherry and captivates a huge audience. |
| 1998 | Writes and performs the FIFA World Cup official anthem "La Cour des Grands" (The Big Event) in France. |
| 2005 | Wins first Grammy Award for best contemporary world music album for Egypt. Sings with Dido in three of the Live-8 concerts that take place around the world—London, Cornwall (England), and Paris. |
| 2006 | Stars in movie Amazing Grace as a former slave who chronicled the efforts of William Wilberforce to end the British slave trade. |

**WEST AFRICAN INSTRUMENTS**
The *kora* is one of the most typical West African instruments. Kora players traditionally come from *griot* families, like N'Dour's. They are storytellers, historians, and genealogists, and pass their skills to their descendants. Dancing and music are inseparable in African cultures, and rhythm is king. Drums used include the *bougarabou* and the *djembe*.

Leather rings on neck move to tune instrument

African *kora*

Kora has up to 21 strings

Leather-covered calabash, *or gourd*

**MOVIE ACTOR**
*Amazing Grace,* a movie that tells the story of the abolition of slavery in 18th-century England, was released 2006. N'Dour played the role of Oludah Equiano, the former Nigerian slave who bought his freedom and made his home in London. There he wrote his best-selling account of his life and fight to end slavery.

Youssou N'Dour as Oludah Equiano in *Amazing Grace*

*"I'm African, yes, but I like to play music for everybody. But my identity is African. That will never change."*

**YOUSSOU N'DOUR**
in an Internet interview, May 2004

**INTERNATIONAL CONCERT PERFORMER**
N'Dour became a household name in 1994 after his smash hit with Neneh Cherry, "Seven Seconds." He has toured the globe for 20 years with his band the Super Etoile de Dakar and has performed with such greats as Paul Simon, Peter Gabriel, Bruce Springsteen, and Sting.

# Milestones in Music

THE STORY OF MUSIC stretches back many thousands of years. It is not just a story of art: the milestones of music also reflect major cultural, political, and technological changes along the way. While instruments and tastes change, people never seem to lose the desire to make music. This timeline charts some of the key moments in the development of music.

Ancient Greek lyre

**c. 9000 BCE**
A Chinese *gudi* (flute) is made from a bird's wing bone.

**c. 4000 BCE**
Harps and flutes are played in Egypt.

**c. 800 BCE**
The earliest known written music is a hymn on a tablet in Sumeria, written in cuneiform (symbols). In Greece, choral and dramatic music develops; wandering musicians called *Rhapsodes* travel from city to city.

**c. 600 BCE**
The Indian *vina* appears. Made from two hollow gourds connected by strings and bamboo reeds, it is the precursor to all hollow instruments.

**c. 550 BCE**
The Greek scientist Pythagoras makes scientific investigations into music to prove that all pitches are mathematically related.

**c. 325 CE**
Emperor Constantine declares Christianity the official religion of the Roman Empire. The spread of Christianity in the western world spurs the development of European music.

**670 CE**
Pope Gregory the Great founds *Schola Cantorum*, the church music school in Rome.

**750 CE**
Gregorian chant (a type of plainsong) is introduced. Used in Roman Catholic church services, it is named in honor of Pope Gregory.

**c. 850 CE**
Western music begins to move from monophony (single melody) to polyphony (two or more melodies at the same time).

**c. 1030 CE**
Guido of Arezzo (991–1033), an Italian monk, develops a method for writing music on a stave, based on the human hand.

Early handwritten church music

**c. 1125**
Troubadours travel through France and Germany, singing secular (nonreligious) songs.

**1454**
Printing is developed by Johannes Gutenberg in Germany. The first printed music comes from Venice, Italy, in 1498.

**1517**
The Lutheran hymnal (book of church songs) is assembled by Martin Luther and Johann Walther.

**1590**
A group of Italian musicians and intellectuals gather in Count Giovanni de Bardi's *camerata* (salon) and experiment with music-drama—early opera. Jacopo Peri's *Dafne* (1598) is the first Italian opera.

**1600**
The beginning of the Baroque period of music.

**1666**
The first signed Stradivarius violins emerge from Antonio Stradivari's workshop in Cremona, Italy. He was a disciple of Nicolò Amati, who made violins in Cremona from 1520.

**c. 1709**
Bartolomeo Cristofori makes the first pianoforte in Florence, Italy. The piano enables the player to play louder and softer notes, which is not possible with its precursor, the harpsichord.

**1750**
Johann Sebastian Bach dies. The end of the Baroque period is often associated with Bach's death. Baroque begins to give way to the simpler styles that mark the Classical period.

**1781**
The first symphony orchestra is formed—the Gewandhaus Orchestra of Leipzig, Germany.

**1786**
Wolfgang Mozart's opera *The Marriage of Figaro* premieres in Vienna. Only three years before the start of the French Revolution, the

opera portrays the social inequalities of the time, much to the discomfort of many in the audience.

**1810**
The Romantic style of music begins to emerge, characterized by music that is less constrained than in the Classical era. Inspiration is derived from literature and nature.

**1830**
Hector Berlioz writes *Symphonie Fantastique*. Subtitled *"An Episode in the Life of an Artist,"* it is regarded as one of the most important pieces of the early Romantic period.

**1839**
The first professional symphony orchestra in the US—the Philharmonic Society of New York—is established. It will later become the New York Philharmonic Orchestra.

**1840**
Franz Liszt uses the term "recital" to describe a soloist's concert.

Slaves riot on a ship to the US

**1848**
The California Gold Rush is at its peak. Stephen Foster writes "Oh Susannah," which becomes one of the most popular songs in the US.

**1862**
President Abraham Lincoln presents the Emancipation Proclamation, ending slavery in the US. The slave trade had brought West Africans to the America, along with their rhythms, songs, and chants. This music is the root of blues and jazz.

**1866**
French composer Jacques Offenbach premieres his operetta (light opera) *La Vie Parisienne*. This is the forerunner of the musical.

**1876**
Wagner's custom-built opera house, the *Festspielhaus*, opens in Bayreuth, Germany.

**1878**
Thomas Edison patents the phonograph, the earliest recording equipment. The first jukebox (a partly automated music-playing device) appears in the US. The word "juke" comes from African-American slang meaning "dance."

**1891**
Carnegie Hall, the first custom-built concert hall in the US, opens in New York.

**1896**
Ragtime enjoys enormous popularity in the US. It predates jazz, and is the first syncopated music to come out of the Americas. It gets its name because the rhythms are "ragged."

**1908**
Arnold Schoenberg publishes his *Book of Hanging Gardens*, which signals in a major change in music composition. The harmonies and tonality characteristic of classical music are replaced by dissonant sounds, creating what many consider to be noise.

**1913**
*Billboard* magazine publishes a list of the most

popular songs in the US. This is the beginning of music charts.

### 1914
World War I begins. The conflict has a profound effect on the arts, and signals a definite end to the Romantic movement.

### 1922
The British Broadcasting Corporation (BBC) is established and brings music to a wider audience.

### 1924
George Gershwin's *Rhapsody in Blue* premieres in New York, commissioned by bandleader Paul Whiteman to bring together jazz and classical music.

### 1928
Kurt Weill and Bertolt Brecht premiere *Die Dreigroschenoper* (*The Threepenny Opera*) in Berlin. Weill brings popular music and jazz into the opera house, and combines it with Brecht's stark writing to create a milestone of music theater. Magnetic tape for recording sound is invented in Germany by Fritz Pleumer.

### 1930s
The first electric guitars are made by the Rickenbacker company, giving guitarists a louder but tonally accurate version of the acoustic guitar.

### 1938
Premiere of the first all-American ballet, *Billy the Kid*, composed by Aaron Copland and choreographed by Agnes de Mille.

### 1942
Benny Goodman and his band bring a new level of recognition to jazz with a concert at Carnegie Hall. Bing Crosby releases "White Christmas," from the movie *Holiday Inn*, and it becomes the top-selling song from a movie. RCA Victor spray-paints Glenn Miller's million-copy-seller "Chattanooga Choo Choo," creating a gold disc.

### 1945
Benjamin Britten's *Peter Grimes* premieres in London, signaling the rebirth of British opera.

### 1948
Columbia Records introduces the 33⅓-rpm LP (long-playing) record in New York. It allows listeners to enjoy 25 minutes of music per side, compared to just four minutes per side on the earlier 78-rpm version.

### 1949
RCA Victor markets the 45-rpm record, the legendary "single."

### 1951
In an effort to introduce rhythm and blues (R&B) to a broader white audience that is hesitant to embrace "black music," disc jockey Alan Freed uses the term "rock 'n' roll" to describe R&B. American Elliott Carter writes his *String Quartet No. 1* and becomes a leading avant-garde (ground-breaking and modern) composer.

Elvis Presley

### 1952
American composer John Cage premieres *4'33"* (four minutes, thirty-three seconds) in Woodstock, New York State. The pianist sits in silence for the duration of the piece. This simple idea—that the sounds around us are part of music—is revolutionary.

### 1954
Bill Haley and the Comets begin writing hit songs. As a white band using black-derived forms, they venture into rock 'n' roll.

### 1955
Lewis Urry develops a small alkaline battery for use in portable sound equipment. The electronic synthesizer is invented by RCA engineers.

### 1956
Elvis Presley becomes one of the world's first rock stars, with his hit "Heartbreak Hotel."

### 1959
US National Academy of Recording Arts and Sciences sponsors the first Grammy Awards (for music recorded the previous year). Berry Gordy Jr. founds the Motown Recording Corporation in Detroit, Michigan.

### 1960
Polish composer Krysztof Penderecki writes *Threnody for the Victims of Hiroshima*, which uses startling new orchestral techniques and notation.

### 1963
The Beatles (John Lennon, George Harrison, Ringo Starr, and Paul McCartney) take Britain by storm. The Rolling Stones (founded in 1962) become the anti-Beatles, with an aggressive, blues-derived style.

### 1969
The first major pop music festival, Woodstock, takes place in Bethel, New York. It stars Janis Joplin, Jimi Hendrix, The Who, Joan Baez, and many others.

### 1970
The French president, Georges Pompidou, asks Pierre Boulez to set up a music research institute.

### 1974
Patti Smith releases the first punk rock single, "Hey Joe." Punk takes hold in Britain in the late 70s, in reaction to the bland music of the day.

### 1976
American composer Philip Glass completes opera *Einstein on the Beach*, the first widely known example of minimalist composition.

### 1979
The Sugar Hill Gang release the first commercial rap hit, "Rapper's Delight," bringing rap off the New York streets and onto the popular music scene. Sony releases first portable personal music player, the Walkman.

### 1982
Michael Jackson releases *Thriller*, which becomes the biggest-selling album in history.

### 1982
The digital revolution begins when the first compact discs (CDs) go on sale.

### 1985
Live Aid, the first international charity concert, takes place in London and Philadelphia. Many prominent musicians and bands perform to raise money for victims of famine in Africa.

### 1987
A group of London-based record labels coin the term "World Music" to describe the mix of African, Indian, and other non-Western music.

### 1998
The first commercial cell phone ringtones are created and delivered in Finland by the cellular operator Radiolinja (now called Elisa).

### 1994
The Fraunhofer Society in Germany releases the first MP3 software encoder, called *l3enc*. Software called Winplay3 is released in 1995, enabling people to play MP3 files (digital music files) from the Internet on personal computers.

### 1999
Shawn Fanning introduces illegal downloading of music, using a program called Napster. Personal MP3 players are available. In 2001 Apple launched their own MP3 – the iPod.

### 2003
The concert hall designed by Frank Gehry for Walt Disney Inc. opens in Los Angeles.

Walt Disney Concert Hall, Los Angeles

# A–Z of Great Performers

THE WORLD'S GREATEST MUSICIANS include performers, not just composers. You probably have your own ideas about the best music and who makes it. Here is a small but wide-ranging selection of music-makers who have either made a lasting impact on the quality of performance or been pioneers in their fields. Whether you agree with the list or not, there is no disputing that they have all achieved something special.

**CLAUDIO ABBADO (b. 1933)**
This Italian conductor's passion for the highest musical standards is matched by his enthusiasm for promoting new music and musicians. He was conducting top orchestras by the age of 30. He was Music Director for La Scala, Milan, has worked with many important orchestras, and took over from the great von Karajan in Berlin.

**LOUIS ARMSTRONG (1901–71)**
The greatest of all jazz trumpeters, Armstrong was born in New Orleans, the home of jazz. He was nicknamed "Satchmo" because of his satchel-shaped mouth. Armstrong gave the solo trumpet an identity all of its own. He also became known as a singer through hits like "Hello, Dolly" and "What a Wonderful World."

**MARIAN ANDERSON (1897–1993)**
A brilliant African-American contralto opera singer, Anderson was denied early recognition because of racial discrimination. In spite of huge success in Europe, she was prevented from performing in Washington, DC. Infuriated, the president's wife, Eleanor Roosevelt, staged a concert for her at the Abraham Lincoln Memorial, which was attended by 70,000 people.

**BEACH BOYS (formed in 1961)**
A pop band formed by three brothers—Brian (chief songwriter and producer), Carl, and Denis Wilson—plus Mike Love and Al Jardine. The Beach Boys created "surf music," with "Surfin' USA," "I Get Around," "Surf's Up," and "Don't Worry Baby." Their only real rivals were The Beatles.

**CHUCK BERRY (b. 1926)**
Berry is probably the most likely candidate for the title of "Father of Rock 'n' Roll." His early hits, such as "Maybelline," "Roll Over Beethoven," and "Johnny B. Goode," are at the root of rock. His talent for fitting a story into a three-minute song made his music and performances irresistible.

**JAMES BROWN (1933–2006)**
This dynamic soul singer set the standard for gospel and funk for five decades. He first achieved success in the 1950s with a string of hits that established him as "Soul Brother Number One." He was known especially for his

The Beach Boys

signature razor-sharp band and the screaming vocals that featured on songs such as "I Feel Good" and "Papa's Got a Brand New Bag."

**MARIA CALLAS (1923–77)**
No one did more to bring passion and glamour to opera than Callas. Known to her admirers as *La Divina* (The Divine), she was admired for her wide repertoire and deeply felt performances. Her voice is the most widely recognized in opera.

**ENRICO CARUSO (1873–1921)**
Born in Naples, Italy, Caruso was the most famous singer of any kind of music in his time. Known as "the tenor's tenor," he dominated the musical world from the stage of New York's Metropolitan Opera.

**BING CROSBY (1903–77)**
The mellow voice and easy delivery of this American popular singer and actor created the "crooning" style of singing. Through his recordings, radio broadcasts, and film appearances, Crosby dominated American pop culture from 1934 to 1954.

**PABLO CASALS (1876–1973)**
Casals was one of the first cellists to promote the cello as a solo instrument. Born in Catalonia, Spain, Casals made his debut at 14, and played for many different heads of state, from Queen Victoria to President Kennedy. He is famous for his interpretation of J. S. Bach.

**RAY CHARLES (1930–2004)**
Charles lost his sight when he was only seven. He was raised on gospel and blues music, and he combined these in his 1955 hit "I Got A Woman." A pianist and vocalist, Charles pioneered his soulful sound in hits such as "Georgia on My Mind" (now the official state song of Georgia).

**MILES DAVIS (1926–91)**
This classically trained American trumpeter, composer, and band-leader was perhaps the 20th century's most influential jazz musician. Davis

was involved in almost all the important postwar developments in jazz, including the early days of be-bop (jazz with a fast tempo and adventurous harmonies).

**GUSTAVO DUDAMEL (b. 1981)**
This flamboyant Venezuelan conductor is a product of his country's inspired music education program, *El sistema* (the system). Thirty years ago, Venezuelan economist and musician Jose Antonio Abreu was alarmed by the number of children living in poverty, so he gave them instruments and music lessons. *El Sistema* now supports 15,000 music teachers, 30 professional orchestras, 150 youth orchestras, and 250,000 students.

Aretha Franklin

**ARETHA FRANKLIN (b. 1942)**
The daughter of an American Baptist preacher, Franklin grew up singing gospel music. Her astonishing run of late 1960s hits earned her the title "Lady Soul."

**VLADIMIR HOROWITZ (1903–89)**
Horowitz is considered one of the most distinguished pianists of any age. His technique and the excitement of his playing are legendary.

**JASCHA HEIFETZ (1901–87)**
Lithuanian-born Heifetz was the supreme violinist of his time. He studied under the maestro Leopold Auer in St. Petersburg, Russia, before moving to the US. Famous for his disciplined approach, he once said, "If I don't practice one day, I know it; two days, the critics know it; three days, the public knows it."

Gustavo Dudamel

**JIMI HENDRIX (1942–70)**
Legendary guitarist Jimi Hendrix was an icon of psychedelic pop. A wizard with a guitar, he was one of the most exciting performers ever to take the stage. Formed in 1967, his group, the Jimi Hendrix Experience, gave unforgettable performances of hits such as "Foxy

Lady" and "Purple Haze," and sang the American national anthem, "The Star-Spangled Banner," at a pop festival. The group broke up after three years.

## KEITH JARRETT (b. 1945)
One of the few jazz pianists at home with both improvised jazz and classical piano, Jarrett has a musical curiosity that knows no bounds, and a technique to match it. Though he has played with jazz giants such as Miles Davis, since 1971, Jarrett has concentrated on improvised solo piano concerts, recording many of them. His classical repertoire stretches from Bach to Arvo Pärt.

## ROBERT JOHNSON (1911–38)
When Johnson wrote "Hellhound on My Trail," he painted a picture of a bluesman outcast from proper society. His recordings are among the earliest and greatest of the traditional Delta Blues of Mississippi and Tennessee.

## JANIS JOPLIN (1943–70)
Joplin made her name fronting the band Big Brother and the Holding Company. Born in Port Arthur, Texas, she moved to San Francisco in the 1960s. Here her career took off with hits like "Piece of My Heart" and "Ball and Chain." Joplin's albums have sold by the millions.

Plácido Domingo

Jose Carreras

Luciano Pavarotti

Luciano Pavarotti often performed with Plácido Domingo and Jose Carreras as The Three Tenors.

Hugh Masekela

## SCOTT JOPLIN (1868–1917)
Joplin is the best-known ragtime composer. Ragtime piano usually uses a syncopated (off-the-beat) melody in the right hand against a straightforward marching rhythm in the left hand. Ragtime was wildly popular during the early 20th century. One of Joplin's best known pieces is the "Maple Leaf Rag."

## FELA KUTI (1938–97)
Kuti was the eccentric, brilliant Nigerian composer, band leader, and founder of "Afrobeat." He used his music as a tool of political protest against the Nigerian military government. He is acclaimed by many artists.

## LED ZEPPELIN (formed 1968)
These British heavy-metal rockers formed the ultimate rock group of the 1960s and 1970s. The band lineup includes the incendiary vocals of Robert Plant, the guitar wizardry of Jimmy Page, the thundering bass of John Paul Jones, and the volcanic drumming of John Bonham. One of their all-time great hits is "Stairway to Heaven."

## MADONNA (b. 1958)
Winner of many Grammy awards, this songwriter, author, producer, and artist has made music history. She has logged an incredible 12 number one pop singles and 35 number one dance singles in the US.

## BOB MARLEY (1945–81)
Reggae is a type of music that combines many styles, but its roots are Jamaican. Bob Marley was the first reggae superstar. He is best remembered for songs such as "I Shot the Sheriff" and "No Woman, No Cry."

## HUGH MASEKELA (b. 1939)
This South African trumpeter is one of the most influential African jazz musicians. He took up the trumpet as a boy, then moved to London in 1960. Masekela opposed apartheid (racial segregation) in South Africa, and his hit "Bring Him Back Home" became Nelson Mandela's anthem.

## JONI MITCHELL (b. 1943)
The model for female singer-songwriters everywhere, Mitchell's unique style of guitar playing and singing was developed in New York in the 1960s. Her classic albums are *Blue*, *Ladies of the Canyon*, and *Spark*.

## CHARLIE PARKER (1920–55)
Nicknamed "Yardbird" or "Bird," Parker was one of the greatest jazz alto saxophonists and composers of all time. A pioneer of "be-bop," Parker was among its most imaginative players, and with Miles Davis and Dizzy Gillespie he led jazz into a new era.

## LUCIANO PAVAROTTI (1935–2007)
The most beloved operatic tenor of his generation, Pavarotti only took up singing after his dream of being a professional soccer player in Italy failed. He conquered the world's greatest opera houses singing works by Verdi and Puccini. He brought Verdi's aria *Nessun*

The Rolling Stones

*Dorma* to millions when he sang it at the 1990 soccer World Cup final in Italy.

## ELVIS PRESLEY (1935–77)
Elvis was born in Tupelo, Mississippi. When he exploded onto the music scene in 1956, nobody had seen anything like his hip-shaking. He drove fans wild with a potent mix of gospel and hillbilly music that became rock 'n' roll. The "King of Rock 'n' Roll" sold an astonishing one billion records worldwide.

## ARTHUR RUBINSTEIN (1887–1982)
A Polish-American pianist, Rubinstein was considered to be one of the greatest piano virtuosos of the 20th Century. He received international acclaim for his performances of the music of Frédéric Chopin and Johannes Brahms, and his championing of Spanish music.

## ANDRÉS SEGOVIA (1893–1987)
The guitar was once considered to be just an instrument for gypsies. Segovia single-handedly rehabilitated the guitar as an instrument to be taken seriously in classical music. He commissioned many original works and transcribed J. S. Bach's lute music for guitar.

## FRANK SINATRA (1915–98)
A showbiz legend, Sinatra redefined popular song. "Ol' Blue Eyes" was the embodiment of a swaggering postwar America at its most confident. Sinatra's voice, together with hits like "My Way," "New York, New York," and "Come Fly with Me," made him the singer of the century.

## ROLLING STONES (formed 1962)
Many consider this to be the greatest rock 'n' roll band in the world. In their early days, the Stones were the rebels and The Beatles were the lovable "moptops." Singer Mick Jagger and guitarist Keith Richards polished their songwriting skills with hits like "Satisfaction" and "Get Off of My Cloud." They were joined by Bill Wyman on bass, Charlie Watts on drums, and Brian Jones on guitar. They have sold more than 200 million albums. The Stones continue to tour and grow old disgracefully.

# Find out more

GETTING INTO MUSIC HAS NEVER BEEN EASIER. No matter what kind of music you like or want to know about, there are plenty of websites to check out and almost certainly performing groups, music schools, and teachers nearby. Just ask around or follow the tips on this page. It is never too early or too late to start; remember that music is about having fun. As the ancient Chinese philosopher Confucius (c. 551–479 BCE) said: "Music produces a type of pleasure that human nature cannot do without."

## USEFUL WEBSITES

The Internet is a great place to start exploring the world of music. You can find information on virtually every aspect of music imaginable, from concerts and composers to downloadable songs and tunes, and advice on how to play an instrument. Some websites even offer lessons in jazz, rock, and classical music. Most large orchestras have their own websites, often with educational pages. Here some useful sources.

- The online encyclopedia Wikipedia has phenomenal music content—just type a name or term into the search window. It will also refer you to other helpful websites. www.wikipedia.org
- This Cincinnati Public Radio site brings Classical music to life through music and stories. classicsforkids.com
- National Public Radio has information on every kind of music, as well as recorded concerts. www.npr.org
- The British Broadcasting Corporation (BBC) runs several orchestras. Its radio stations broadcast everything from Handel to hip-hop, and it has an archive going back 50 years—much of it available online. www.bbc.co.uk
- Listen to music from the British Library's sound archive. www.bl.uk/
- For beginners taking their first steps in digital music, createdigitalmusic.com and tweakheadz.com

### GO TO CONCERTS
Live music of any kind can be very exciting. To find out about musical events near you, look in the local paper or online. There is usually a choice of concerts by amateur classical performers, choirs at churches and schools, or local bands. Professional orchestras and choirs put on a range of concerts to suit different interests and levels of experience. Many have special daytime concerts designed to appeal to young people.

### JOIN A CHOIR
Wondering which instrument to start with? Why not start with your voice? Getting together with 20, 60, or 100 others to sing can be a truly uplifting experience. As well as being great fun, all that breathing is good exercise. You will experience music first-hand and often get to work with orchestras. It is also a great way to meet other kids who are crazy about music too.

### LEARN TO PLAY AN INSTRUMENT
Everyone loves the chance to strum, blow, scrape, or hit something and have music come out of it. Guitars and pianos are the most popular instruments, but there is nothing like playing your first tune on a saxophone or clarinet. Ask at your school, or find out from local music clubs what instruments they have, and when you can try them out. You will be surprised how easy it is to get started.

# LISTEN TO MUSIC FROM MORE GREAT COMPOSERS

• **HECTOR BERLIOZ (1803–69)**
A French Romantic composer, Berlioz revolutionized the sound of the orchestra with his instrumentation. His most famous piece remains his diabolically inventive *Symphonie Fantastique*.

• **GEORGES BIZET (1838–75)**
In a life cut short by overwork, this French composer created one of the great operatic masterpieces, *Carmen*. This glorious score changed the course of opera writing with its realistic, passionate portrayal of a defiant gypsy girl who works in a cigarette factory.

• **BENJAMIN BRITTEN (1913–76)**
Britten was the most dominant and prolific 20th-century composer His music influenced every part of British musical life. He reinvented British opera for the 20th century and his *Young Person's Guide to the Orchestra* is many people's initiation to orchestral music.

• **FRÉDÉRIC CHOPIN (1810–49)**
A Polish composer, Chopin was one of the early Romantic piano virtuosos. All of his work includes the piano in some role, usually as a solo instrument. Chopin's piano music is considered to be the pinnacle of the pianist's repertoire. The *Funeral March* and his *Minute Waltz* are his most famous pieces.

• **CLAUDE DEBUSSY (1862–1918)**
This French pianist and composer's musical vision brought European music into the 20th century. His *Prelude à l'Après-Midi d'un Faune* (Prelude to the Afternoon of a Faun) and *La Mer* (The Sea) were pioneering orchestral works.

Frédéric Chopin

• **EDWARD ELGAR (1857–1934)**
England's greatest composer since Henry Purcell was largely self-taught. Elgar's orchestral works include the *Enigma Variations*, the *Cello Concerto*, and the *Pomp and Circumstance Marches*. He also composed oratorios, chamber music, symphonies, and instrumental concertos.

• **MANUEL DE FALLA (1876–1946)**
De Falla was the greatest Spanish composer of the 20th century. He brought the colors and drama of Spanish folklore to life with his vibrant compositions, which included many ballets and operas. His *Ritual Fire Dance* and the dances from *La Vida Breve* (Life is Short) are among de Falla's most thrilling works.

• **CHARLES IVES (1874–1954)**
Ives was an ingenious pioneer of early American orchestral and vocal music. He made his living selling insurance, while devoting his spare time to writing music. Ives wrote many wonderful songs based on American folk melodies and hymn tunes.

• **LEOŠ JANÁČEK (1854–1928)**
This Czechoslovakian composer did not achieve success until in his fifties. The operas he wrote after that, such as *Jenůfa* and *Kát'a Kabanová*, thrillingly combine the folk music and speech patterns of his native language to produce intense dramas.

• **FELIX MENDELSSOHN (1809–47)**
Born into a wealthy German family, Mendelssohn was a composer and pianist. He wrote beautiful, gracious music. His *Violin Concerto* and the *Wedding March* from his music for Shakespeare's *A Midsummer Night's Dream* are regularly performed.

• **GUSTAV MAHLER (1860–1911)**
This Austrian Romantic composer wrote huge symphonies, songs, and song cycles. A famous work, the *Adagietto* from *Symphony No. 5*, was used in the film *Death in Venice* His *Symphony No. 8* required 1,030 musicians for its 1910 premiere in Munich, Germany.

• **JACQUES OFFENBACH (1819–90)**
Offenbach created the French operetta—light opera with singing and speaking. He wrote nearly 100 delightful pieces. His *Orpheus in the Underworld* is best known for its famous *Can-Can*. He also wrote a popular opera, *The Tales of Hoffmann*, based on the children's stories of E. T. A. Hoffmann.

• **CARL ORFF (1895–1982)**
Orff was a prolific German composer. Despite his enormous output, his reputation rests on one very popular work, *Carmina Burana*. Its famous chorus, *O Fortuna* (Oh Fortune) has been used in movies and on television—even in aftershave advertisements. Orff's lasting influence is his lesser-known work as a music educator.

• **COLE PORTER (1891–1964)**
American composer Cole Porter wrote some of the cleverest and funniest songs to grace the Broadway stage. He wrote shows like *Kiss Me Kate*, *Anything Goes*, and *Silk Stockings*. His style and wit are the standard to which composers and lyricists aspire. Porter's most famous lyrics are: "Birds do it. Bees do it. Even educated fleas do it. Let's do it, let's fall in love."

John Williams composed the film score for the blockbuster movie *Star Wars*.

• **HENRY PURCELL (1659–95)**
Purcell was one of England's most important and original Baroque composers. He worked during the reign of three monarchs. He composed odes (musical poems), sacred anthems, songs, opera, and chamber music. The Rondo from *Abdelazer or the Moor's Revenge* was used by Britten in his *Young Person's Guide to the Orchestra*.

• **A. R. RAHMAN (b. 1966)**
Many Indian pop songs come from the hundreds of movie musicals made there. Rahman is one of India's most successful film composers. Trained in both western and Indian music, he has sold over 100 million records. Rahman wrote the musical *Bombay Dreams*, produced by Andrew Lloyd Webber.

• **GIOACCHINO ROSSINI (1792–1868)**
Rossini was the greatest Italian comic-opera composer of the 19th century. In all, he wrote 39 operas, and each one bubbles with fun. His orchestral writing whips up a frenzy of excitement. Rossini's most popular works are *The Barber of Seville* and the overture to *William Tell*. Rossini was so successful that he was able to retire at the age of 37.

• **FRANZ SCHUBERT (1797–1828)**
Schubert's short life bridged the Classical and early Romantic music eras. His gift for a great melody is apparent in everything he wrote. His works include symphonies, piano sonatas, chamber music, and 600 songs.

• **STEPHEN SONDHEIM (b. 1930)**
American composer and lyricist Stephen Sondheim has redefined the Broadway musical with his witty lyrics and surprising plots and characters. In 1957 he wrote the lyrics for Leonard Bernstein's *West Side Story*. Since then, Sondheim has written both music and lyrics for 15 shows.

• **JOHN WILLIAMS (b. 1932)**
Willliams, an American, is the most popular film composer working today. He has written many famous scores, including those for *Star Wars*, *E. T.*, and *Harry Potter*. Williams has won five Academy Awards and was principal conductor of the Boston Pops Orchestra.

# Glossary

**A CAPPELLA** An Italian phrase that means "in the style of the chapel." It describes a piece written for voice(s) without instruments.

**ALTO (OR CONTRALTO)** The lower female singing voice below the soprano.

**ARIA** A piece of music sung by a solo singer, with or without orchestral accompaniment.

**ARRANGEMENT** The adaptation of a piece of music or a song into a form that is different from the original composition.

**ATONAL** Music that does not have a tonal center (see Key), or in which all notes are given equal importance, resulting in eerie and surprising sounds.

**BAROQUE PERIOD** Music composed from about 1600 to 1750. The name comes from the Portuguese word *barroco*, used to describe ornamental jewelry. Baroque music is very ornamental and embellished. The period was also characterized by the introduction of opera.

**BASS** The lowest male voice, below the tenors. It is also the name for the lowest instrument in the string family, the double bass, and the lowest sound or instrument in a piece of music.

**BRASS** Made of metal, these are the loudest group of instruments in an orchestra. From highest to lowest, they include trumpets, horns trombones, and tubas. Sound is produced by blowing hard into a mouthpiece. Brass instruments are an important element of jazz.

**CANTATA** This is Italian for "a piece to sing." It is a work performed by soloists, choir, and instruments, often in a church service.

**CELTIC** This refers to the culture of Celts, people who come from Ireland, Scotland, and Wales. Remnants of Celtic culture also exist in northwestern France, northern Spain, and Portugal.

**CHAMBER MUSIC** Music composed for small groups, usually a *duo* (two players), *trio* (three), or *quartet* (four), although there can be up to eight musicians. Chamber music was originally performed in a small room.

**CHOIR** A group of singers. The choir is usually divided into four voice types. From highest to lowest, they are: sopranos (trebles), altos, tenors, and basses.

**CHORAL MUSIC** Music sung by a small or large group of singers. Choral music is sometimes accompanied by instruments.

**CHORD** Two or more notes sounded together to create a harmonious sound.

**CHOREOGRAPHER** A person who creates dance routines and movement sequences for dancers and other performers.

**CLASSICAL PERIOD** This is the period in music that started around 1750 and lasted until about 1820. The symphony, string quartet, and concerto forms all evolved during this period. Its main composers were Haydn, Mozart, and Beethoven. "Classical music" is often used to describe music played by orchestral instruments.

**CONCERTO** A piece for soloist(s) and orchestra. The Italian word *concerto* means "playing together." A piano concerto features the piano with orchestra, and a violin concerto the violin. All are designed to show off the soloist.

**CONCERTO GROSSO** This is the Baroque era's version of the concerto. It uses two groups of instruments, one larger than the other, which alternate in playing the music. The two groups are the *ripieno* ("full" in Italian) and the *concertino*.

Conductor

**CONDUCTOR** A person who directs a group of instrumentalists or singers, such as an orchestra or choir.

**CONSERVATORY** A place to study music. It is also sometimes known as a *conservatoire.*

**COUNTERPOINT** A combination of two or more independent tunes played against one another in a way that sounds tuneful.

**COVER VERSION** In popular music, a cover version, or simply a cover, is a new performance or recording of a previously recorded song.

**FUGUE** A composition form in which a theme is introduced by one voice, and then copied by other voices. The Italian word *fuga* means "fleeing," and in a *fugue* one voice "chases" another.

**HARMONY** This is created when three or more notes sound together in a chord. When chords sound in succession (one after the other) this is also called harmony or a harmonic progression.

**IMPRESARIO** A term used in the entertainment industry for a producer of concerts, tours, and other music events.

**IMPROVISATION** The art of composing music while performing it, without the use of written music. In an improvised piece, the musicians "make it up" as they go along.

**INSTRUMENTAL MUSIC** Music written for instruments, without vocal accompaniment.

**JAZZ** An American musical art form that originated around the beginning of the 20th century in the southern United States. It used a mix of African and European music traditions. Jazz has evolved into many different styles, including swing, be-bop, and Dixie.

**KEY** The tonal center of a piece of music, based on the first note (or tonic) of the scale. A key signature on a stave tells a musician which notes to play in a piece of music. The word key also refers to an individual note on a piano or keyboard.

Jazz saxophone

**LIBRETTO** The text that is sung in an opera or oratorio, written by a librettist.

**LITURGICAL MUSIC** Music used as part of church worship (liturgy).

**LYRICS** The words to a song. A lyricist is the person who writes lyrics.

**MADRIGAL** A type of secular (not religious or sacred) song popular in the Renaissance period, especially in England and Italy. Madrigals were usually sung without instrumental accompaniment, and often used the words of a love poem.

**MASS** The main service in the Roman Catholic Church, comprising specific sections performed in a set order: *Kyrie, Gloria, Credo, Sanctus, Agnus Dei,* and *Dona nobis pacem.*

Girls' choir with altos and sopranos

**MELODY** A series of notes that create a tune or theme.

**MONOPHONIC MUSIC** Simple, unaccompanied music sung by a one person or a group. It was common in the Middle Ages.

**MUSICAL** An abbreviation of "musical theater," this is a kind of show that tells a story using songs, dialogue, music, and dance.

**OPERA** Musical theater played out with singing and orchestral accompaniment.

**OPUS** This is a Latin word meaning "work" and is used when cataloging a musician's pieces. It is often abbreviated to "op." and followed by a number to show the order in which it was published. Beethoven's Symphony no. 5 is op. 67, meaning that it was the 67th piece he published.

**ORATORIO** Works performed in concert halls by solo singers, choirs, and orchestras, usually based on a Biblical text. Oratorios use the same musicians as operas, but the singers do not wear costumes and there are no stage sets.

**ORCHESTRA** A large group of musicians—sometimes more than 100—playing together. An orchestra uses the four categories of instruments: strings, woodwind, brass, and percussion.

**OVERTURE** A short piece of music played at the start of an opera or musical to familiarize the audience with the important melodies. Many overtures have become so famous that they are performed in concerts, such as Gioacchino Rossini's *William Tell Overture*.

**PERCUSSION** A group of instruments that are struck, shaken, or scraped. Orchestral percussion includes timpani, cymbals, drums, and xylophones. Although these instruments have been around for many thousands of years, it is only in the last century that they have been widely used in orchestras. Percussion is an essential feature of pop music, rock, and jazz.

**PITCH** This describes how high or low a note is in the musical scale. It can refer to a specific pitch, like "middle C" on a piano, or be general—the top note on the violin is a very high pitch, whereas a tuba's bottom note is a low pitch.

**PLAINSONG** Unaccompanied singing in church music using the lowest, or bass, voice. Gregorian chant, named after Pope Gregory the Great, is a well-known type of plainsong.

**POLYPHONIC MUSIC** Polyphony literally means "many sounds." It refers to vocal or instrumental music in which all the parts are independent and of equal importance.

**PRELUDE** A short piece of music without any specific form that introduces a longer and more substantial piece. Bach wrote 48 *Preludes and Fugues*, in which the fugues were introduced by the preludes. Frédéric Chopin used the prelude form for solo piano pieces, while Wagner wrote preludes to his later operas instead of overtures.

**QUARTET** A group of four instruments. The most common form is the string quartet (two violins, one viola, one cello).

**RENAISSANCE** Roughly spanning the period from the 14th to the 16th centuries, the Renaissance (from the French word meaning "rebirth") was a historical period marked by a revival of interest in learning and the arts. In music, the period was marked by the development of harmony. Instrumental and secular vocal music were popular.

**REQUIEM** A Mass for the dead, performed in the Roman Catholic Church. The word *requiem* is Latin for "rest."

**ROMANTIC MUSIC** The Romantic period took place from about 1820 to 1900. Music was often based on a poetic or literary source and usually told a story. Some of the most famous Romantic pieces are Hector Berlioz's *Symphonie Fantastique* and Franz Liszt's *Faust Symphony*.

**SAMPLE** A short extract from an existing recording that is used in a new recording. The screams of soul legend James Brown and the drummers of the Motown label recordings are among the most sampled pieces.

**SCALE** A series of notes that define a tune and, usually, the key of the piece. Different scales give music a different feeling and "color."

African drum

**SECULAR MUSIC** Nonreligious music written outside the church. It was the earliest kind of popular music. In the Middle Ages it included instrumental music used for dancing, love songs, and folk songs.

**SONATA** Italian for "sound piece," a sonata is an instrumental piece for soloists or groups of instruments, with three or four movements (sections). Sonatas were often written for piano, or for solo instruments accompanied by the piano.

**SOPRANO** The highest female singing voice.

**STAVE (OR STAFF)** The grid of five horizontal lines on which music is written.

**STRINGED INSTRUMENTS** A group of instruments in which strings are bowed and/or plucked. From smallest to largest, they include violin, viola, cello (or violoncello), and double bass. Strings are the largest part of an orchestra.

**SYMPHONY** Derived from ancient Greek, this word means "sounding together." A symphony is a piece for a large orchestra, usually in four movements (sections).

**TENOR** The highest male voice, above the basses. The word tenor can also be used to describe instruments in that same sound range, such as the tenor saxophone.

**TONE POEM** Also called a symphonic poem, this is a piece of orchestral music in one movement that tells a story. The story may come from a poem, novel, or painting. It was very popular with the Romantic composers.

**TREBLE** The highest male voice, or the highest instrument or part in a piece of music. Also the name for the symbol (clef) used to indicate notes above middle C on the piano.

**VIRTUOSO** A brilliant musical performer. Nicòlo Paganini and Franz Liszt were famous historical virtuosi, while modern examples include Maxim Vengerov and Evgeny Kissin.

**WIND INSTRUMENTS** Instruments in which sound is made by blowing into a mouthpiece. From highest to lowest they are piccolos, flutes, oboes, clarinets, saxophones, and bassoons.

Percussion section

Wind section

Brass section

String section

The typical layout of a modern orchestra

# Index

# Acknowledgments

Dorling Kindersley would like to thank: Steve Setford for copy editing, Stewart Wild and Constance Novis for proofreading, and Hilary Bird for the Index. Christine Heilman for Americanization; David Ekhom-Alburn, Claire Ellerton, Sunita Gahir, Susan St. Louis, Lisa Stock, & Bulent Yusuf for the clipart; Claire Ellerton & Susan St. Louis for the wall chart.

Music provided by Royalty Free Music Library.

The publishers would also like to thank the following for their kind permission to reproduce their photographs:

a-above; b-below/bottom; c-center; l-left; r-right; t-top.

Ali Akbar College of Music (www.aacm.org): Lawson Knight 50tl; akg-images: 19tc, 22-23bc, 24bc, 29c, 30c; Beethoven-Haus, Bonn 20br; Stefan Diller 9bc; Marion Kalter 53cr, 54tl; Erich Lessing 7cr, 17tl; Nimatallah 7tl; Michael Teller 8bc; Alamy Images: Peter Adams Photography 33crb; Ambient Images Inc. 44cra; Arco Images 10cr, 15tr; Bildarchiv Monheim GmbH 14tr, 15cla; Frank Chmura 53cl; Content Mime International 56cb; CuboImages srl 10tl; David Davis Photoproductions 62bc; Dinodia Images 51br, 59cr; Mary Evans Picture Library 13br, 20cr, 28cl, 28tr, 69c; Frederick Fearn 55tl; Robert Fried 28br; Robert Harding Picture Library Ltd 9tl, 47l; imagebroker 4bl, 22tl, 31tr; INTERFOTO Pressebildagentur 25tl, 38tr; Lebrecht Music and Arts Photo Library 44tc, 47c; Mirror-7 Arts / 25br, 27cl, 27tr, 29cra, 30tl, 32cr, 32tl, 34tl, 35ca, 36bc, 39br, 40tl, 47br, 49ca; Photos 12 57cr; Pictorial Press Ltd 19cr,

20tl, 35crb, 37tl, 42c, 43br, 57tr, 59cb, 61cra, 62cr, 65tl; Popperfoto 23tl, 60cra; Stephen Saks Photography 50cra; Visual Arts Library (London) 2cra, 12tl, 18tl, 21cr; Peter Widmann 23br; The Art Archive: The British Library, London 50bc; Claude Debussy Centre, St Germain en Laye / Dagli Orti 54c; Galleria d'Arte Moderna, Rome / Dagli Orti 26tl; Liszt House, Weimar / Dagli Orti 23tr; Museum der Stadt, Wien / Dagli Orti 23cb, 38tl; Museum of the City of New York 41cl; Private Collection 26tr; Bournemouth Symphony Orchestra: Chris Zuidyk 71br; The Bridgeman Art Library: The British Library London 18crb; Coram Family in the care of The Foundling Museum, London 13cb; Nationalgalerie, Berlin 22c; Private Collection 8-9bc, 9cr; Private Collection / Bonhams, London 26c; Private Collection, Archives Charmet 25cr; Corbis: The Art Archive 17br; Asian Art & Archaeology Inc. 55tc; Morton Beebe 32bc; Bettmann 10br, 12bc, 13tc, 28tl, 36cr, 43tr, 44cl, 45tl, 46bc, 59tl, 62tr; Henry Diltz 66tr; EPA / Angel G. Medina 16br; EPA / Fabrice Coffrini 51bl; EPA / Guenter R. Artinger 21bl; EPA / Juan Carlos Cardenas 55cr; EPA / Sigi Tischler 66br; The Gallery Collection 29tl; Hulton-Deutsch Collection 41cr; Robbie Jack 15c, 27bc, 30-31b, 37b, 41b; Kipa / David Lefranc 31crb; Marvin Koner 36tl; Richard T. Nowitz 7br; Panchout 53tr; Neal Preston 52tl, 61tl; Reuters / Fred Prouser 67cl; Reuters / Jeff Vinnick 67tr; Reuters / John Schults 62tl; Reuters / Nir Elias 29br; Sunset Boulevard 48tr; Sygma / Matsumoto Toshi 55b; Sygma / Tony Frank 60tl; Underwood & Underwood 37tr, 58l; Zefa / Svenja-Foto 14tl; DK Images: Archaeological Receipts Fund (TAP) 7cl; Courtesy of The Boston Symphony Orchestra 35cb; Courtesy of The British Library, London / Laurence Pordes 3cb, 64bc, 64-65 (Background), 66-67

(Background), 68-69 (Background), 70-71 (Background); The British Museum, London 64cl; Courtesy of the Anthony Barton Collection 4tl, 9tr; Courtesy of The Imperial War Museum, London 39clb; Judith Miller / Cooper Owen 60cl; Judith Miller / Linda Bee 44bc; Judith Miller / Thos. Wm. Gaze & Son 3tr, 67br; Judith Miller / VinMagCo 49tl; Judith Miller / Wallis and Wallis 2cla, 59br; Rough Guides / 13tr, 65br; Courtesy of The Science Museum, London 29cla, 58cr; Getty Images: AFP / Catherine Ashmore 57b; AFP / David L. Pokress 33bl; AFP / Harcourt 56c; Allsport / IOC Olympic Museum 35cra; Erich Auerbach 48crb; The Bridgeman Art Library 16c; Fox Photos 58b; Dave Hogan 61b; Hulton Archive 40bc; Hulton Archive / Keystone 58c; M.J. Kim 63br; Liaison / Cynthia Johnson 60bc; New York Times Co. 54bc; Michael Ochs Archives 42tl, 66c; Patrick Riviere 19tr; Adam Rountree 57tl; Ian Showell 49tr; Time Life Pictures 46c; Time Life Pictures 33bc; Time Life Pictures / Anthony Verde 61cl; Time Life Pictures / Eileen Darby 48tl; Time Life Pictures / Eliot Elisofon 42br; Time Life Pictures / Herb Snitzer 45br; Time Life Pictures / Pix Inc. / Jerry Cooke 33tl; Roger Viollet / Lipnitzki 52c; The Kobal Collection: 20th Century Fox 45bl, 45tr; 20th Century Fox / Lucas Film 69br; Magna Theatres 45c; Mirisch-7 Arts / United Artists 49b; Sovkino 47c; Universal 41tc; Warner Bros 35bl; Lebrecht Music and Arts Photo Library: 11cr, 17bl, 17cr, 20clb, 21tr, 27cr, 31tc, 39cr, 39tr, 43tl, 44tl, 46tl, 52br, 53bc; L. Birnbaum 19bc; C. Christodoulou 18bc; ColouriserAL 21br; Richard Haughton 21tl; Tristram Kenton 11bl, 24-25bc, 34br; Matti Kolho 34cb; S. Lauterwasser 13cl; Laurie Lewis 38b; Ric Mahoudeau 47tr; John Minnion 22bc; Odile Noel 70bc; Neale Osborne 36tr; Rodgers & Hammerstein Org 44crb;

Graham Salter 19l; Chris Stock 41tr; Library Of Congress, Washington, D.C.: 5tr, 10bc; NASA: 33tc; Redferns: JM International 63tl; Rex Features: Everett / C. Goldwyn 63cr; Bill Robinson 56tl; Geoff Robinson 14-15bc; Still Pictures: Argus / Peter Frischmuth 68cl; Transit / Peter Hirth 68cr; Teatro alla Scala: 26br; V&A Images: Poster from 'Umrao Jaan', a film by Muzaffar Ali 51br; Wikipedia, The Free Encyclopedia: 2clb, 6c, 8tr, 43tc

Wall chart: akg-images: Stefan Diller fcla (monks). The Art Archive: Galleria d'Arte Moderna Rome / Alfredo Dagli Orti ftr (Verdi). The Bridgeman Art Library: Nationalgalerie, Berlin, Germany fbl (Liszt). Corbis: Hulton-Deutsch Collection cb (Bernstein); Robbie Jack ca (Tamara Rojo); Underwood & Underwood crb (Beethoven). DK Images: Palau de la Musica Catalana, Barcelona clb (Beethoven); Rough Guides fcra (ballet); The Science Museum, London tc (phonograph). Getty Images: clb (violin); Eliot Elisofon / Time Life Pictures c; Cynthia Johnson fcra (Dylan). Redferns: bc (NDour).

Jacket: Front: Alamy Images: Mary Evans Picture Library (tl). The Bridgeman Art Library: Private Collection (tcl). Corbis: Claus Felix / dpa (tcr). DK Images: Commodore Records / Verve Records / Universal Music Group (ca, Billie Holiday record). Back: Alamy Images: Imagebrokers (tl); Peter Harrison (cr). Corbis: Bettmann (c); David Lees (bc); Underwood & Underwood (br). Redferns Music Picture Library: David Redfern (cl).

All other images © Dorling Kindersley
For further information see: www.dkimages.com